PERSONAL

RECONSTRUCTION

PERSONAL RECONSTRUCTION

FIRST EDITION

A PSYCHOLOGICAL, SPIRITUAL, FINANCIAL AND LEGAL COURSE

IN THE ART OF PREVENTING PERSONAL CRISES,

AND RECOVERING FROM THEM

Peter Tarlow, Ph.D.
Tom Marrs, Ph.D.
Nathaniel Tarlow, J.D.
Eduardo Leite, Ph.D.

Quest Publishing ❖ *Miami, Florida*

Inquiries should be directed to :

Quest Publishing
2655 S. Le Jeune Road, Suite 500
Coral Gables, FL 33134 U.S.A.
Tel. +1 305.779.3069 • Fax +1 305.901.2120
email: editor@quest-publishing.com

ISBN-13: 978-0-9769416-1-3
ISBN-10: 0-9769416-1-9
Library of Congress Control Number 2017963676

Editor: Jacques Island

First Edition: January 2018

10 9 8 7 6 5 4 3 2 1

Visit us on the web at quest-publishing.com

To police officer and constable Calder Lively,
who lives each day working to help human beings
avoid the pitfalls of life and
when necessary to reconstruct their lives.
Calder is an inspiration to all who know him.

Contents

List of Figures

List of Exercises

List of Tables

Foreword

As the proverbial sayings go, self-help books are "a dime a dozen," but "they are not all created equal."

This one, I think, stands out because it is truly practical, and no one author tries to cover subject matter beyond their hard-gained expertise. Here, we have a team of four authors—practicing experts in religion, psychology, finance, and law—cooperating to produce a holistic book on managing the curveballs that life can pitch at us in various epochs of our lives: the teen years, at midlife, and in our retirement.

Of course, we are children before we are teens; we are young adults before we reach midlife, and we normally work decades before we can reach retirement age (if we are fortunate).

Personal crises are usually related to one of these epochs, but they can also befall us during the years that precede any of them. For example, a thirty-something man can experience early midlife crisis issues, or a relatively young woman who contracts an incapacitating illness may find herself dealing with anxieties and traumas normally associated with the retirement years.

The authors of this book coined the term in-visioning as a concept to help readers understand the conditions that can lead to life's crises and to act preemptively. They also provide the tools for reconstructing our lives when we do suffer a crisis. These are the before and the after phases of a crisis, respectively.

We have organized this book in a way to make it easy for readers to absorb and implement its lessons, which include descriptive narratives about each topic, exercises to excite your thoughts and motivate action, figures to illustrate concepts, and related appendices for use on your own or as a participant in a workshop.

We welcome your feedback about this book's usefulness in reconstructing your life or, if you are a workshop leader, the lives of your participants. Our aim is to publish improved editions according to the comments, observations, and suggestions we get from readers and individual or group practitioners of the methods presented in this book.

Despite their years of practice in helping people reconstruct their lives, the contributors to this book never cease to wonder at how each and every case reveals new twists and insights about the human condition and the unique paths that individuals take to move forward to a better life.

Jacques Island
Chief Editor

Introduction

In 1966 Dan Greenberg and Marcia Jacobs (1987) published a book entitled *How to Make Yourself Miserable*. Greenberg's and Jacob's book was meant as a tongue-in-check work to teach people that being alone and miserable was perhaps not the best way to live.

Unfortunately, all too many of us at times seem to be Ph.D.'s in misery, or what we might call "miserology." At times, all of us find ways to ruin our finances, go afoul of the law, make psychologically wrong decisions and often live spiritual lives that appear to be "Eclipses of God."

When we make wrong choices, when we decide to ignore our best instincts we often "crash" with reality. Just as in a car crash, we too need to reconstruct the scene of the accident so that we are able to reconstruct our lives and get on with the chore of living.

This book can be a complementary textbook for instructors covering subjects that include personal crisis management. It is not meant to be a mere self-help work. Instead, it seeks to help you see where you crashed, what errors were made and how to avoid these same mistakes in the future.

ON GOD AND PERSONAL RECONSTRUCTION

As you work through this book you should take our references to God to mean *your* notion of who or what God is, or is not. Almost all of us already have an understanding and belief system about this notion. This book does not intend to change your notion of God.

Also, the references are not to discuss theology or compare religions, or to proselytize any particular faith; but we do include some fables, and parables from ancient times and scriptures, that we think make good points for our discussion about in-visioning and recovery from personal crises.

THE GENESIS OF THIS BOOK

Our inspiration for this work comes from our consulting services to police agencies around the world. They know that after an accident they must reconstruct the accident, learn what went wrong and determine fault.

Police often spend time with citizens reassuring them that an accident is not the end of the world. Yes, there will be blame and the potential for compensation, or even imprisonment in some cases, but any police officer will tell people at an accident that as long as there is life there is hope for recovery and reconstruction.

AUTO ACCIDENTS AS A METAPHOR FOR PERSONAL CRISES

According to police reports, human error causes about 99% of all the accidents. What is true of car accidents is also true of human accidents. Just as in the world of auto accident investigation, we need to ask hard questions when reconstructing the crises and crashes that occur in our lives. Among these questions are the following:

- Can we reconstruct the problem?
- How did our personal accident occur?
- Were other people involved in causing the accident?
- Were other people casualties because of the accident?
- Was this accident a unique event in your life or a reoccurring event?

As in the case of vehicle accidents, in life many if not most of our personal accidents happen when we are not paying attention; when something hits us from nowhere; or we are someplace in time or space where we should not be. So in personal reconstruction we also need to ask additional questions:

- What signals did we miss?
- Do we see the signs along the way?
- Were we going too fast in life?
- Were we up against something bigger than us?
- Were drugs or alcohol involved?
- How did we come out damaged?
- How did others get damaged?
- What is unique about our demographic? For example, what are the problems specific to our age group?

This book is meant as an aid to help you avoid the accidents of life, to learn from them and assure that they do not reoccur. As in a traffic accident, we often are in such a hurry to get somewhere in life, to accomplish a goal that we speed forgetting to ask some circumstantial questions:

- Am I speeding through life and taking unsafe shortcuts?
- What is my personal situation in life and who might be hurt were I to fail?
- What is the condition of my path in life?
- Can I react quickly or am I so stuck in my sense of self that I cannot see an accident coming?
- Am I capable of changing direction?

When a police officer looks at an accident reconstruction, the investigator takes every possible variable into account. That is what this book is about, It reminds us to contemplate how often and how close are these items to the accident.

IN-VISIONING YOUR ROUTE THROUGH LIFE

To help you assess the conditions of your life's path to avoid accidents, and to gather the tools needed for reconstruction when you experience a crash, we have developed a methodology that we call "in-visioning."

Just as the word implies, in-visioning allows us to see ourselves from an outside perspective, to look into our lives and to develop those skill sets that will permit us to understand past mistakes and avoid future pitfalls.

HOW THIS BOOK IS ORGANIZED

We have divided this book into four parts and nine chapters and supporting materials, as follows:

Part I contains the three chapters that deal with *in-visioning* the crash, "the art of the before and the after"; in other words, knowing what is in front of you and how to avoid the crash before the impact.

Part II is about *reconstructing* the crash, understanding why you did not see it coming and learning how to avoid future crashes. And, because personal crashes are often "driven" by at least one of life's four major activities — our personal finances, our legal issues, our mental health, and our spiritual well-being — we have devoted specific chapters to these four drivers.

Part III contains a capstone chapter to help you draw lessons from the exercises in the previous chapters, summarize where you have been, and easily formulate your action plan to move forward into the future.

Part IV is the section where you will find appendices and information that are better outside the narrative chapters.

■ ■ ■

This book is less than a comprehensive treatment in personal reconstruction but it will teach you skills in the main aspects of life that can help you avoid crashes and pull yourself together from the crashes you cannot avoid. Still, there are situations for which this book is not intended and for whom it is *not* meant:

- This book cannot magically pull you out of bankruptcy
- This book cannot repair a broken heart.
- This book cannot end your drug addiction or get you to stop smoking.
- This book cannot replace a lawyer.
- This book cannot make your spouse love you.
- This book cannot assure you of admission to heaven.

What we offer is a system to get you to a good state of "personal maintenance" to avoid the road hazards; and, "repair tools" to help you fix accidental damage you did not avoid.

PART

I

IN-VISIONING

This section introduces the concept of in-visioning, who this book is for, and provides an overview of "The Before" and "The After" phases of personal crises.

C H A P T E R

1

THE ESSENCE OF IN-VISIONING

Be brave enough to live the life of your dreams
according to your vision and purpose instead of the
expectations and opinions of others.

— Roy T. Bennett,
"The Light in the Heart"

A LL OF US spend a great amount of time looking at other people. How we appear to others often impacts not only our own self-image, but also many of our life outcomes. For example, numerous academic studies have shown that good-looking people are, on the whole, more successful in business. Most of us are, of course, experts in seeing what others may be doing correctly or incorrectly, though we may be less effective at seeing our own faults.

In life, we see others but only a reflection of ourselves. The best that we can hope for is to see a mere reflection of ourselves either physically, as in a mirror, or verbally from what others tell us about ourselves.

This book is all about helping you to see yourself as you are so that you can avoid one or more of life's crashes. It is a tool through which you can reconstruct your life after a personal crisis or crash.

WHAT IN-VISIONING IS AND IS NOT

We cannot emphasize too often that this book is neither meant to replace a psychological professional such as a therapist, nor will it solve all of your spiritual, financial advising, or legal needs. Instead, this book—and the art of in-visioning, broadly—is meant to teach you how to ask the right questions and discover what areas in your life need to be corrected.

In-visioning is meant to help you see yourself in the way that others may see you, specifically from four key perspectives. Each of these aspects of life—the financial, legal, psychological, and spiritual—is intertwined with the other aspects and tells us a great deal about how others see us and what we need to know about ourselves. As such, in-visioning is more than merely the sum of its parts; it is a methodology for knowing yourself, seeing yourself in the ways that others see you, and helping yourself to avoid life's accidents or prevent crashes before they occur.

"…in-visioning…is meant to teach you how to ask the right questions and discover what areas in your life need to be corrected."

In-visioning assumes that God has made each of us to be unique creatures who share our communal humanity, and that our lives are unique and different from all other lives. It focuses on how we are alike and yet different from others whom we know.

The reason that we focus on all four aspects of life is that each aspect interacts with the others. To look at any one aspect alone is, in the long run, to invite failure.

THE FOUR BASIC ASPECTS OF LIFE

The four basic aspects of life in which people often "crash"—no matter which of the many sociological cohorts they may belong to according to their age, gender, ethnicity, or economic status—are the financial, legal, psychological, and spiritual aspects of life. Most people's personal accidents occur when one of these four aspects suffers a breakdown.

In essence, in-visioning helps us to perform a personal reconstruction that touches each of these four disciplines. Specific aspects from each of these disciplines may be combined, making each field (the combination of aspects) unique. As you continue to read, you will see how personal reconstruction is like, and unlike, the worlds of finance, law, psychology, and spirituality.

Two of these aspects—the spiritual and the psychological—often manifest themselves through legal or financial problems. Just because we do not see these problems, however, that does not mean that they do not exist. Very much to the contrary, psychological and spiritual diseases are the silent killers of our well-being, of our careers, or of our personal lives. For example, many a marriage ends because of monetary disputes, but if we carefully analyze these disputes, we will see that money troubles may well be the manifestation of a deeper problem.

Figure 1.1 shows the relationship between these four fields in which the two top fields—psychology and spirituality—refer to the softer disciplines, and the bottom fields—finance and law—are what may be called the harder fields. The circle represents personal reconstruction, where the four blend.

Figure 1.1. Four aspects of personal reconstruction

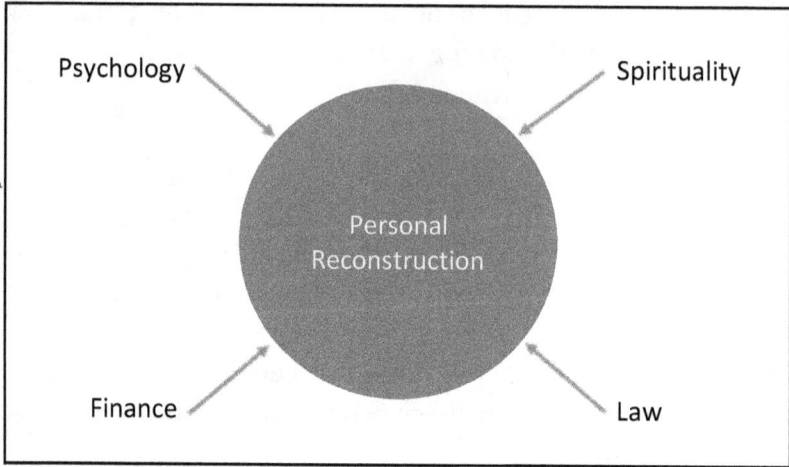

Psychology

This field is based on the assumption that there is, to use the Kabbalistic phrase *olam ha'nistar*, a "hidden world" in which we operate. Psychologists often disagree about the field in which psychology operates. Some psychologists take us into a world of indirect self-discovery; others tend to be more directive. In reality, there is no singular psychology but rather a group of related fields that work under the assumption that people control much of their lives, and that human beings are capable of change when they desire to change.

Spirituality

Like psychology, spirituality often means different things to different people. In fact the whole notion behind spirituality is that there are no mathematical mysteries to human life. The way in which we are in touch with our spiritual side is both personal and unique.

Spirituality distinguishes the human being's existence from

that of the machine. It assumes a non-zero-sum game in which, as each person's spirituality increases, the total spirituality also increases. In contrast to a legal or financial battle, spirituality has no losers. However, finance and law are zero-sum games in which there are finite outcomes and one person's win is another's loss.

Finance

The world of money entails choosing what we do and do not desire to acquire in life. How we view money tells us a great deal about who we are.

Finance is also about winning. It assumes that life is a zero-sum game and that, given an even playing field, the person with the most brains and willingness to work will probably win. Finance is somewhat mathematical in that correct decisions are made by an analysis of data. Finance also assumes continuous use of evaluation methods to determine what worked and what did not, how we give value to a product or service, and which values match reality's demands. In like manner, personal reconstruction assumes that people evaluate their lives.

No one has everything in life, and so personal reconstruction demands of us that we assign values to our priorities. However, a business' *raison d'être* (reason for being) is often easier to determine than a human being's. Often, we are not sure what our priorities are, and without this knowledge, goal setting and evaluation become difficult if not impossible.

Law

Law assumes the existence of a right and a wrong, and like finance, it assumes that life is a zero-sum game. Law may or may not be connected to morality and exists both inside and outside of the real world.

Lawyers often compare their profession to a battlefield: there is an opposition and a battle plan, a winner and a looser. Law is both black and white, and it is filled with nuances and inferences. A good lawyer assumes that it is his or her job to defend a client's interests. In fact, many European languages use some form of the word *advocate* to refer to lawyers. Lawyers are, then, often less interested in "the truth" than in just representing a client's position.

Law lives within its own parameters, which are often distinct from what is often called *common sense* or even *morality*.

KEY ASSUMPTIONS

This book assumes certain things about the human condition. If you disagree with these assumptions (and that is your right), then this book and its methods are probably not for you. In partifular, this book works through the following four key assumptions:

1. **How we handle our money is an insight into how we live our lives**. Too many people believe that finances are divorced from life's realities. This book's authors disagree. You do not need to be an expert in finances and you do not need to be rich, but how you handle your money is an exterior manifestation of your inner life. When boiled down to its simplest denominator, money is nothing more than a form of simulated energy. In other words, it represents the value of energy as translated into a numerical term. We learn a great deal about human beings by how they choose to earn money, spend money, save money, and invest money. Some of us are satisfied with minimal sums of money, and others need a great deal more. Some are willing to make great sacrifices in its pursuit, and others place their priorities elsewhere. Insights into our finances teach us a great deal about who we are and are not, what our fears are, whom we care about, and what our hopes and dreams may be.

2. **Our views about the law reflect our views about life.** Just as with money, how we choose to live within or outside the law teaches us much about who we are. None of us live entirely within the law. Most people find ways to bend the law, and too many of us are quick to enforce legal codes that apply to others and demand leniency for ourselves. Often, life crashes occur when we choose to speed down life's highways and ignore the legal signals along the way.

3. **People can change.** Assuming that a person desires to turn his or her life around and has the proper guidance and motivation, psychological health is obtainable. We do not accept the notion that all is predestined, that people are not responsible for their own actions. This book operates under the assumption that people can make wise decisions along the way and that their decisions will often determine the outcomes of their lives.

4. **Human beings are the product of a force that is greater than they are.** The reader may choose to call this force "God" or by whatever name she chooses. The notion that human beings have no responsibility to each other and to this force beyond themselves is alien to the ideals behind this book.

For reasons of simplicity, we are calling this force "spirituality." We derive this term from the Hebrew word *ruach*, which refers to both intangible motivations in life such as love and to the tangible side of action, such as the wind.

Because Hebrew is a more abstract and spiritual language than English is, often a Hebrew word will be adapted to English usage. By "spirituality in human reconstruction," we are referring to the Hebrew term *teshuvah*, which has no English equivalent but may be translated as "a sense of spirituality in which and by which humans are capable of taking personal life inventories of seeing their flaws, of building on their strengths, of correcting mistakes, and of turning their lives around."

Doing *teshuvah* means asking the necessary questions in order to avoid and learn from crises so that they do not reoccur.

WHOM THIS BOOK IS INTENDED FOR

Although anyone can benefit from personal in-visioning, this book is especially useful for four separate groups of people, both before and after a personal accident. The group descriptions that follow clarify why we have focused on these particular groups.

Teenagers

Before a personal accident, this is the group that does not listen.

After a personal accident, this group of people often makes more poorer personal choices that result in both legal and financial difficulties.

Inmates

Before a collision, inmates made poor choices.

After a collision, individuals in this group need to reconstruct their lives. Starting again is never easy.

Midlife-Crisis Sufferers

Before a personal crisis, people in this cohort throw away much of their success because of feelings of ennui

After a personal crisis, too many of these people (especially men) tend to be lonely, alone, broke, and confused.

Individuals in Retirement

Before a personal crisis, people in this group have many fears: How will I recover? Do I have enough? Am I running out of time?

After a crisis, these are people who often feel warehoused and lonely. Abandoned and without friends, they face existential crises of the first magnitude.

■ ■ ■

In summary, this chapter examines the purpose of in-visioning and whom it aims to help overcome, or at least cope with, roadblocks in their lives—your life!

As we said at the start, the advice given here will not perform miracles; righting your ship and setting it back on course to relief or happiness takes a lot of work and determination on your part, but this book can serve as your navigation chart. You can do it just as so many others before you have.

Lao Tzu, an oft-quoted ancient philosopher, once wrote:

The thousand mile journey
begins with the first step...

To that famous saying, we would add: ". . . any step within your personal journey."

CHAPTER

2

THE BEFORE

Look at what you want to change, gather a few
people who believe in it like you do, and start moving
forward....[Y]ou don't always need a destination.
Sometimes, you just have to make forward motion.

— Debby Ryan

HOW OFTEN HAVE we wished that we had seen an accident coming? Police officers will tell us that although in some cases mechanical failures may be responsible for an accident, most accidents stem from human failure and are very much avoidable. For example, while at a marriage ceremony, we may wonder whether the couple is really prepared for marriage. And how many parents have told their children that they are headed down a wrong path and, although they pray for their offspring's success, question the wisdom of their life choices?

All too often, the person involved in the crash has asked him or herself, "How come if my friends saw it coming, no one said anything to me about it?" The odds are that they did see the accident coming and did say something but the accident's participant chose not to hear.

It should be noted that this book does not use the term victim. The authors assume that in most cases, we are not the victims of personal crashes but rather are participants in them. Given a bit more insight and willingness to be aware of what life is telling us, most of us are able to see and understand.

To answer the kinds of questions that you might ask yourself about a crash, imagine yourself driving down a road. What are some of the questions that you might ask yourself? For example, you might ask questions such as these:

- What do I see?
- What dangers lurk ahead?
- How clear is my vision?
- How well am I paying attention to the road?
- With what other vehicles or objects might I collide?
- How tired am I?
- Do I have any physical or mental impediments?
- Am I going at the right speed?
- Is my mind clear, or am I under the influence of drugs or alcohol?

Now apply these questions to your own life's journey.

THE RISKS OF DRIVING DOWN LIFE'S HIGHWAY

To be alive is to assume risk. Life's risks begin even before birth. From the moment of conception, we are responsible for only part of what happens to us in life. In fact, some of life's most important aspects are decided for us at conception. We not only have no control over our genetic makeup, but also who we are, which is determined to a great extent by factors outside of our range of control. For example, the color of our skin, our native talents, and even our God-given gender are personal character-istics over which we have no control.

In like manner, the types and quantities of food that our mothers consumed while we were in their wombs, the amount of prenatal care that our mothers received, and even how our fathers treated our mothers are factors that are well beyond our control but that influenced our characteristics.

Figure 2.1. Risk continuum

High Risk Takers   Risk Adverse

Risk involves everything from crossing a street to starting a new business. Some risks are self-chosen. For example, sharing a bed with another person is a risk, marrying that person is an even greater risk, and choosing to bring a new life into the world is perhaps the greatest of these personal risks.

Naturally, not all risks are the same, and were we never to assume any risk, then we would not be able to continue living. It is necessary, then, in managing risk—the "before" of a personal accident—and understanding why a crash occurred, to develop a deeper understanding of your own risk relationship. Are you a risk taker or are you risk adverse? Are you afraid of all or even some risk? Or do you tend to see life as a series of risk challenges not only to meet, but also to add spice to life and make it worth living?

Most of us spend most of our lives in the middle of the "risk continuum" (Figure 2.1). However, personal crashes occur when we misjudge risk. That is when the potential for failure is greater than our ability to handle a risk.

To complicate the problem, each of us judges what a "success" or "failure" is. One person may find a failed marriage to be devastating, although another person may see a failed marriage as an opportunity for a personal renaissance. How a risk is interpreted, then, is as much an issue of personal preference as it is a mathematical formula.

In-visioning Your Life

The foundation of this book rests on what you want your life to be like from this moment forward. The first exercise encourages you to in-vision a future for which you can create a road map to get to your in-visioned life.

Figure 2.2. In-visioning for family worksheet

Major Question	Minor Questions	Life Journey Risk	Guiding Principle
What type of family life do I want?	Where should we go on vacation? Join school PTSA?	Finding myself alone in life	I value family life over other activities
Do I seek a job or shall I start a business?	How much time do I want to work?	Becoming a workaholic	Be a good provider for my family
What is the role of God in my life?	Do I like the spiritual leader at my place of worship?	Seeking only immediate rewards	Spirituality grounds me
How important is money to me?	What gadgets do I wish to buy? Why?	Money accumulation overtakes all else	I and my family need money but not an excess
How do I achieve peace of mind?	Do I like myself? Do I care for others?	Emotional instability and reputation loss	Act so others are proud of me, and be charitable

Your personal circumstances may pose extraordinary difficulties, but a better life is ahead if you set your mind to it. Working through the exercises in this book will give you the elements that you need to live your vision.

Be sure to give this chapter—as the first step toward personal in-visioning and reconstruction—a lot of thought, because it sets up broad, guiding principles to the other exercises in this book.

Figure 2.2 shows an in-visioning worksheet that has been completed by someone who is focused on family life over other considerations, and Figure 2.3 is the same worksheet that has been completed by someone who is focused on wealth creation. Although all of us need to ask some common questions, each of us also has a number of personal values to address.

Figure 2.3. In-visioning for money worksheet

Major Question	Minor Questions	Life Journey Risk	Guiding Principle
What type of family life do I want?	How much time will family take from me? Do we have to vacation?	Family can get in the way of other interests	Family life is important but so are other interests
Do I seek a job or shall I start a business	How much time do I want to work?	A job limits how much I could make	Money sustains me/my family, so it comes first
What is the role of God in my life?	How can God help me get out of my predicaments?	What if I dedicate time to God and there is no God?	If I show religion others will think better of me
How important is money to me?	What gadgets do I wish to buy? Why?	My hard work may not be rewarded enough	Wealth is my proof of success over others
How do I achieve peace of mind?	Do I like myself? Do I care what others think?	Peace of mind could be costly with specialists	Live for myself and not for others

Note that the two foregoing illustrations have the same major questions. The worksheets diverge in terms of the personal perspectives of two very different individuals, each of whom in-visions different life paths that lead to very different expected outcomes—their guiding principles.

We provide these two divergent examples to highlight that different individuals have different values, even when they seem to agree about most things. Our purpose in this comparison is to point out that your in-vision is just that: uniquely yours.

People's motivators and values can focus on many factors other than family or money. Perhaps your concerns are represented among the following major questions:

- How important is my freedom?
- Can I be productive with my new disability?
- Is sobriety important to me?
- Do I enjoy my gambling habit?

You will benefit from being honest with yourself. And you will benefit the most if you are contemplating a personal reconstruction because you are not satisfied with your current life. If that is your situation, then this exercise is exactly what you need in order to rethink your values and guiding principles.

Exercise 2.1. In-vision your life

Go through the following steps using the blank worksheet, found in Appendix A.1 on page 146:

1. In the left column, list between three and five "Major Questions." These are philosophical statements about your values. If they apply to you, then you may use questions that appear as examples in this chapter, or you may list your own questions.
2. In the "Minor Questions" column, list more-specific questions that relate to a major question. Your minor questions should articulate how a major question can be applied to real life through action.
3. In the third column, "Life Journey Risks," note one or more possible negative consequences to the question that

could prevent you from realizing positive benefits from your major and minor questions. Risk awareness is risk avoidance.
4. Finally, the fourth column for "Guiding Principles" is what you expect and want your major questions' outcomes to be.

This final step—producing guiding principles—is most important, as these principles form the framework for your newly in-visioned life.

Assessing Personal Risks

Now that you have in-visioned your new life, you will want to identify and assess the personal risks that you can expect will work against your plan. Risks create stress, and everyone has personal risks—some of less consequence, and others that could prove severely hurtful if not mitigated or managed successfully.

Figure 2.4. Personal risk assessment worksheet

Type and Description of Risk	Risk Level	Expected Duration
Looming divorce. Two years married and with one child to support	3	1 year
Career change. Stuck in end-job and need to increase income to maintain 2 households	2	3 months
Credit card debt. Two credit cards with $7,000 balance – difficulty paying $200/mo. minimum	5	No end with current income
Education loan. Being pressured for monthly $100 payments since dropped out of college	5	5 years
2015 DUI arrest record that's impacting my job prospects	1	5 more years

In our second exercise, we will use three variables to assess your personal risk type, level, and duration. This will alert you to the dangers that you need to mitigate as you work to achieve your in-vision. These are the mines in the field that you need to cross.

Exercise 2.2. Create your personal risk assessment

You can now complete your own personal risk assessment like the one illustrated in Figure 2.4. Begin by referring to Table 2.1 to begin understanding your own concept of risk tolerance and to decide what levels of risk to assign to each of your entries into your assessment worksheet using Appendix A.2 on page 147.

Table 2.1. Risk levels and their effects

IMPORTANCE	PROBABILITY	CONSEQUENCES
Level 1	High	Highly negative
Level 2	Moderate	Highly negative
Level 3	Minimal	Highly negative
Level 4	High	Significantly negative
Level 5	Moderate	Significantly negative
Level 6	Minimal	Significantly negative
Level 7	High	Slightly negative
Level 8	Moderate.	Slightly negative
Level 9	Minimal	Slightly negative

You may at first have trouble finding examples of all nine types of risk within your life's context. Take some time to think about these issues. Part of personal in-visioning entails taking the time to think about your life, what might go wrong, and how to fix it before it goes wrong or, after the event, what did go wrong and how to fix the circumstances surrounding the event so that such events do not happen again.

Note that the foregoing nine categories do not deal with the question of consequence duration. For example, a short-term severe consequence may in some cases be more tolerable than a long-term middle range consequence. Duration is considered along with risk type and level and is noted in the worksheet.

Remember to answer the following questions for yourself; do not worry about what another person may think unless others' opinions are part of your risk plan:

- What are your top three personal risks?
- What are your top three financial risks?
- What are your top three social risks?
- What are the three major risks to your personal reputation?
- What are your top three health risks?
- What three things do you do that might be considered risky?
- Where in your life are you risk-adverse?
- How well do you tolerate others' risk taking?
- What are three risky things that you have done in the past year?
- What are three things that you have not done because you thought that the risk was not worth the potential reward?

Keep in mind that determining something to be a personal risks is a subjective assessment. One person's severe consequence may be a minimal consequence in the mind of another.

You can learn a lot about yourself by looking at the types of questions that you ask. In-visioning teaches us that wisdom comes from the quality of questions that we pose, and knowledge comes from the quality of the answers that we have received.

Factors That Lead to Human Collisions

Having completed your in-visioning and risks worksheets, now let us consider five key variables in a human collision.

First, what is your speed through life? The title of David Hale Sylvester's (2012) book *Traveling at the Speed of Life*—used in a recent advertisement—may be considered just a bit too cute as a phrase. But it does emphasize that too many of us are traveling through life so quickly that we fail to see the bumps along the road. For example, our children may be crying out for our help, but because of the stresses of everyday life, we simply fail to notice. However, some of us are traveling through life at speeds that are so slow that we put others and ourselves at risk. A major mistake that often puts us on a collision course is over-caution.

Just as in driving, some of us suffer from analysis paralysis. Do you over- or under-analyze? Are you in such a rush to finish that you overlook many an important detail? Or are you so detail oriented that you accomplish precious little?

Second, are you physically up to your desired speed? Another component to analyze about getting through life is your body's capacity. Our bodies are fine machines. Everyone, however, has some physical limitations. Do you take care of your body? Do you fuel it properly? Do you give your body the rest and workout that it needs?

Often, we forget that our mental state is connected to our physical state. If we are aching, underfed (or overfed), and lack proper nutrition, then we are heading toward an accident or life-course collision. Just as many an accident is caused by improper vehicle maintenance, our proper bodily maintenance also facilitates personal accident avoidance.

Third, what are life's "weather conditions" through which you are traveling? Although many experts, psychologists and clergy push for personal responsibility, this is not always the case. Malcom Gladwell (2013) points out in his book *Outliers* that much of what happens to us is outside of our control. Who we are often depends on the sex and race into which we were born, our family's status and wealth, and even the time during which we are alive. Although these external factors are often outside of our control, knowing what they are and how we can use them to the best of our abilities is very much within our range of control.

This book does not seek to solve the "nature versus nurture" debate, but it does borrow from each and integrates ideas from both sides of the academic argument.

Fourth, how quickly can you react to change? When driving, we need to be alert to changes on the road. An animal may suddenly appear, a child may run into the road, or an oncoming car may swerve off and into our lane.

Good driving means that the driver has to be quick on his or her feet. In like manner, our voyage through life demands that we learn to react rapidly to ever-present changes.

In life, all things are in a state of change. The issue is not whether we can hold back the tides of change, but rather how quickly we can either control life's changes or adapt our life's patterns to change. It is essential to remember that you do not have to like change and that not all change is for the better. What you must be able to do is adapt to the never-ending changes that encompass life. Remember, life is not a static noun but a dynamic verb.

Fifth, can you change directions? Once you know that you can live with or tolerate change, it is essential to determine how well you adapt to changing conditions. Changing the course or direction of one's life is never easy. This book is about change and what we need to do to accept changes, which are ever in a state of perpetual occurrence.

What other human factors did we miss? Especially in the before, remember that there are always factors that you will miss. Good risk management is all about understanding that you will never eliminate all risk. Instead our goal needs to be about how we can lower risk and learn to lessen its impact.

Personal reconstruction means understanding that in all aspects of life, risk is ubiquitous. To illustrate, a lawyer never really knows how a jury will decide, and despite claims to the contrary, no one has ever been to the afterlife and returned to tell about it.

Determining which risks we choose to manage is another clue into how we can prevent life accidents and what to do about them when we need to reconstruct our lives in the post-accident phase.

Concentrating on The Before

Often, theology, spirituality, and physics seem to come together. For example, the laws of thermodynamics tell us a great deal about personal reconstruction and the act of in-visioning.

Thermodynamics' first law is that "energy can be changed from one form to another, but it cannot be created or destroyed" (Farabee 2001). This law certainly applies as much to a personal accident as it does to a vehicle accident. We are all composed of energy. Some of us use that energy for positive reasons, and others for negative reasons. The trick, then, is not to lessen the energy but to convert it for positive gain.

The second law of thermodynamics reminds us that all order is open to entropy; in other words, that order, unless maintained, will become disorder. Once again, what is true in physics is also true in life. Even the best of us tend toward disorder. Personal in-visioning provides us with the breaks for our own personal entropy. It is a means of holding on to life's order and converting disorder into order.

The laws of thermodynamics are also reflected in some of the great theological debates. For example, if God created the world *ex nihilo* (out of nothing), then what existed prior to creation? On one side of the debate are the Aristotelians who argued that cre-ation was ever present, that nothingness has simply never existed. The opposite position is that God created what we call creation from out of nothing.

Although philosophers may still debate this seminal question, how we define our beginnings certainly determines the depth and correctness of our analysis. Often, this search for accurate beginning points—commencement points—set the context for understanding where we went off course and what we need to do to in-vision our errors and begin the long, arduous task of per-sonal reconstruction.

To complicate our task further, we need to wonder whether time always flows in a unidirectional path. That is, does the past (i.e., the beginning) always precede our future, or can time flow in a multidirectional manner? Which of the two diagrams in Figure 2.5—A or B—do you think best represents temporal reality?

Figure 2.5. Concepts of temporal reality

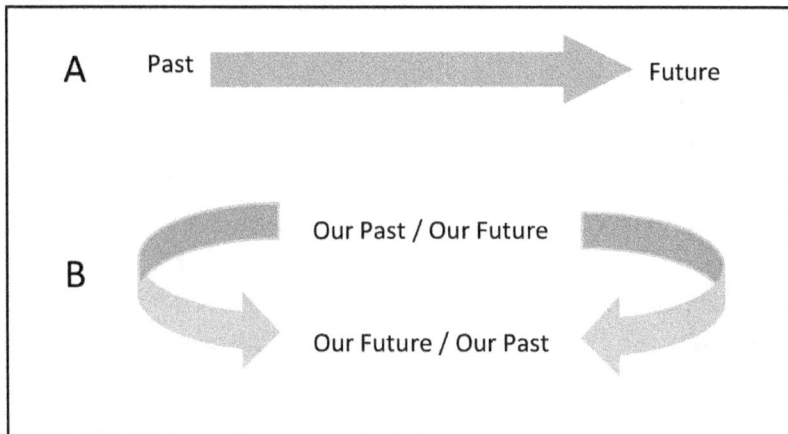

In other words, is there an interaction between our past and our future? Do we live in the present or is our present nothing more than the mathematical point where past and future meet? This eternal riddle forms the essence of this book.

FACTORS THAT AFFECT THE BEFORE

It should not be surprising that what we choose to surround ourselves with—that is, what we wear—reflects us; it can affect future outcomes even when they seem to be innocuous. What do the following points of discussion tell us about you and your journey through life?:

Clothing. Most people understand that our clothing often acts as a statement to others about who we are or are not. However, we tend to forget that what we choose to wear also reflects our own inner moods and ought to tell us something about who we are and where we are going.

Footwear. When driving, our footwear is important. In our life voyage, our life support is our footwear. Are we on a firm footing in life? How might we trip ourselves? Do we tie our life's laces well, or are there all sorts of laces that never seem to get tied in our lives?

Packages. When a pedestrian has a car accident he is often so concerned about what he is carrying that he does not pay attention to the road. In life we are all carrying "baggage." How we carry our personal baggage often tells us a great deal about who we are and how we are heading for a crash. Are you carrying baggage that does not permit you to see the road ahead? Are you so blinded by the past that you are failing to see the future?

Eyewear. Often, a person's first reaction when involved in an accident is: "I never saw it coming!" How alert are you to crises that are coming down the pike? Do you have sufficient foresight? Are you choosing not to look because you fear seeing something that you might not like?

These questions are essential in personal reconstruction. Remember that personal reconstruction is not a psychology course, nor is it a substitute for professional financial, legal, psychological, or spiritual advice. Personal reconstruction is a course that is developed to help you avoid a crash before it happens and to recover from it, should it happen. Finally, this course is meant to be hard work as well as fun.

Before we go on to the next chapter, take time now to ponder these key terms and questions:

- Do I know who I am?
- Have I taken the time to do a personal inventory that includes my financial health, my legal status, my psychological health, and my spiritual state of being?
- Of the four aspects of life—financial, legal, psychological, and spiritual—which is the most important for me?
- Of the four aspects of life—financial, legal, psychological, and spiritual—which one forms the basis for the other three?
- Why are so many of us more perceptive about other people's lives than we are about our own?
- Do I know where my blind spots are? How do I compensate for these blind spots?
- How aggressive am I in my life's travels?
- Am I traveling through life at the proper speed?
- Why is traveling at the wrong speed dangerous?

■ ■ ■

In summary, we have learned that our personal problems often begin long before they are manifested. The best way to solve a problem is to avoid it. Thus, through an understanding of our finances, our role in society, and our psychological and spiritual states, we can shape a better tomorrow and avoid future problems.

In this chapter, you established your own in-vision—how you want to live your life and what your values and priorities are—and you identified the risks and potential obstacles in your path to that vision.

We now close this chapter with a final checklist for avoiding crises that you may want to refer to occasionally.

WAYS TO AVOID A CRISIS

1. Live your own life, not one comparing yourself to the accomplishments of others.

2. Don't seek or rely on external validation.

3. Follow your own path when you can. (Don't try to please everyone.)

4. Look for positive people and positive thoughts.

5. Dare to try new things.

6. Avoid worrying about the past or future. Focus on the present.

7. Think about the kind of person you want to be, and take steps in that direccion.

8. Avoid taking things personally. Most things that seem directed at you are not.

9. Don't worry about little things. (And almost everything is a little thing.)

10. Accept the kindness of others.

11. Extend kindness to others.

C H A P T E R

3

THE AFTER

You build on failure. You use it as a stepping stone.
Close the door on the past. You don't try to forget
the mistakes, but you don't dwell on it. You don't
let it have any of your energy, or any of your time,
or any of your space.

— Johnny Cash

I N CHAPTER ONE, we explained the concepts of in-visioning and personal reconstruction. And chapter two emphasized "the before"—the necessary precautions to take to avoid a personal accident. This revolved around the theme of getting control of our lives, of accepting responsibilities for our actions, and realizing that many of life's less-than-happy moments can be avoided. We may or may not be responsible for having caused the accident but, in the end, the accident still occurred, and we have to deal with it. Despite our best efforts to avoid risk, however, accidents do happen. We lose our jobs because of a downturn in the economy. A family member gets unexpectedly sick. We enter a new stage of our lives and experience a hormonal change. Our house burns down, and all our most precious possessions literally go up in smoke.

This chapter presents the other side of the coin—the "after." It is not about assigning blame but about recovering, and its goals are threefold:

1. Understand and assess what took place
2. Deal with the problem
3. Determine what you can learn from it so that the occurrence does not happen again.

This chapter is also your opportunity to begin your reconstruction by creating some initial tools using the inventory worksheets. The completed worksheets from this chapter, and others in subsequent chapters, will guide you through the process of reconstruction.

We have also noted whom this book is for: people in their adolescence, people who have run afoul of the law, people entering a midlife crisis, and people entering their post-work years. Now we look at these same cohorts but from the perspective of an event that has already occurred. Seen from this perspective, our goal is to understand the "was" and learn from it so that it does not become another "will be." We will examine the psychological and spiritual sides and then seek to understand them from the financial and legal sides of the crash.

FACTORS THAT CAN HOLD YOU BACK

Post-accident in-visioning can be complicated because it requires that we be honest with ourselves and with others. Honesty is difficult during successes and even more difficult during failures. We all have a tendency either to blame others or to be too hard on ourselves. Yet blaming oneself or another does not solve a problem. It only masks the problem in such a way that we learn nothing from it and are prone to repeat it.

The following sections describe the factors that most often get in the way of an honest analysis.

Issues of Guilt

The number of jokes told about guilt ought to tip us off to guilt's power as an emotion. In the sections dealing with psychology and spirituality, this emotion will be dealt with in much greater detail. For the moment, it suffices to say that whenever a negative occurrence happens, there is some form of guilt confrontation. These confrontations tend to take place in one of three ways, as discussed below.

Total denial of guilt. Simply put, this is when we say that something is "not my fault." For example, this chapter's author, Peter Tarlow, has spent years working with federal prison inmates. In almost all cases, inmates at first claim that they are in prison by mistake. Only after they feel comfortable with a counselor and their own situation are they willing to admit that they may have had something to do with their having gone to jail. Denial, then, is a powerful tool that works against personal reconstruction. It is always easier to blame someone or something else. The problem with denial is that we learn nothing from it.

Tendency to over-emphasize guilt. Too many of us blame ourselves for everything. The bottom line is that not everything bad that has ever happened is your fault! To believe that you are responsible for all evil is to give yourself a sense of control that simply is not accurate. You do control some things, but you do not control most things. People who have this sense of guilt need to examine what it is that makes them believe that they control more than they do. In other words, yes, you made a mistake, but life will go on, and somehow you will find your way back into it.

Motivational guilt. This is guilt that is either imposed from within or from without and is temporary in nature. Motivational guilt exists to make you do something that you may simply not wish to do. For example, let us assume that a child does not want to go to college. Her parent has saved for years and given up countless pleasures to allow the child to attend a university. If the child gives in to the parent's pressures and decides to go to college, then the motivational guilt has accomplished its task and fades away. If, however, the guilt fails to motivate the victim properly, then it may turn to anger or into a higher level of guilt. Interestingly enough, suicide is often a form of guilt inducement. Suicide, however, rarely has a long-term guilt impact and turns a temporary problem into a permanent tragedy.

Ideas of Nostalgia

Nostalgia can cause us to look back when we should be looking forward. There is no biblical word for nostalgia, but there is a biblical story that teaches us a lot about what happens when we look back.

Genesis speaks of the destruction of Sodom and Gomorrah. The only family that is permitted to leave the cities before God destroys them with fire and brimstone is Lot's. They are permitted to escape under the condition that they do not look back. Lot's wife, however, cannot help herself. She looks back, and then becomes a pillar of salt. Although the story may be nothing more than a legend, it teaches us a great deal. Looking back can make us bitter, and the moral is that once something has happened, we must be smart enough to let go.

There is a significant difference between remembering and looking back. We define remembering as the act of learning from the past so as to correct a mistake or to build on a success. To look back, however, is to be mired in the quicksand of time. It is to fail to go beyond our mistakes and to create a new future for ourselves. It is, rather, to dwell in the past and refuse to move on. This is the world of "if only I had . . . " or the world of what Arthur Freeman and Rose DeWolf (1990) call the "woulda, coulda, shoulda."

In-visioning means going beyond merely regretting past mistakes and missed opportunities; it teaches us to remember our past but not to get caught up in it, to learn from the past and not to repeat it.

All of us at one point or another make mistakes. All of us wish that we could redo history, but if we continue to blame ourselves for past mistakes, then we relive them in a virtual, self-created hell. There is a difference between regretting that something has occurred and being afraid to move on. Often, this stasis—such as that which was experienced in the Bible by Lot's wife—is connected to a negative form of nostalgia.

Table 3.1. Restorative and reflexive states of nostalgia

NOSTALGIA TYPE	RESTORATIVE	REFLEXIVE
Stress	Action of going home	The longing
Push for Homecoming	Quickens it	Delays it
Way it thinks of itself	Truth and tradition	Faces modernity
Dealing with absolutes	Protects the absolute truth	Questions absolute truth
Politics	National revivals	How do we inhabit two places at the same time
Emphasis on	Symbols	Details
Memory	National and linear	Social and varied
Plots	Restore national origins and conspiracy theories. A paranoiac reconstruction of "home" based on rational delusions	Past is dealt with irony and humor. Mourning mixed with play pointing to the future

Source: Boym (2001), ch. 4, 5.

Nostalgia usually does not carry a pejorative connotation. In fact, the term was first used as a medical term in Switzerland and was taken from two Greek words: nostos, meaning "to return home," and algia, meaning "a longing for." Often, however, nostalgia and progress are a bit like Robert Louis Stevenson's (2017) Jekyll and Hyde characters: nostalgia is not merely an expression of local longing, but a new understanding of time and space that make the divisions of "local" and "universal" possible.

The information in the chart in Table 3.1 was first developed for political purposes, but here it is adapted and applied to "the after" side of in-visioning.

Notice that there are some people who seek to restore that which was. The problem with attempts at restoration is that they fail. There are others who enter into a reflexive mode. If these people can learn from their personal reflections and then move on, then this mode can be very useful. However, there are others who simply reflect on their past but do nothing to change their future. We might call this modus operandi the "dead hand of history."

THE MODERN AND POSTMODERN WORLD

Beginning with celebrated writers such as Jean Baudrillard, Jacques Derrida, and Jean-Paul Sartre, to name just a few, modernity merged with postmodernism. This book is not a philosophical treatise or a literary study, but we shall look, if only superficially, at one small part of postmodernism—namely, the idea that every culture has its own value and that each person can set his or her own moral compass in life.

The problem with postmodernism is that although it appears to be democratic, in reality its tolerance breeds both conflict and intolerance.

Postmodernism also provides us with no guidelines. If everything is equal to everything else, then nothing stands for nothing—that is, we would have fallen into an ethical black hole in which questioning becomes a prohibition in a world without prohibitions.

Many of us have grown up in this postmodern "I'm OK, you're OK" world of absolute relativism. The problem is that as long as everything is going right, there are no crashes, and the system appears to be working. But when things begin to go wrong, then there are no standards to fall back on.

Exercise 3.1. Learn from former crises

Now, think about issues that you have had in your life and what ethical, spiritual, psychological tools you used to help yourself climb out of the abyss. Figure 3.1 is an example of this exercise. Use the blank worksheet found in Appendix A.3 on page 148 to create your list of crises.

Figure 3.1. Former life crises worksheet

Crisis	Tools I Used to Get Back On My Feet
My wife/husband left me	Found support groups, went to bank and reorganized finances, sought out clubs and other places so as to not dwell on my anger
I lost my job	Went to unemployment agency and got assistance for six months, went to employment agencies to search for new job, used family and friends to expand network
My children left home and I felt like an empty nester	Got psychological help for my severe depression, became active in organizations, took up dancing and gourmet cooking

POST-ACCIDENT PRINCIPLES

So far, the exercises have focused on helping you take stock of your past, character, and circumstances to enhance your awareness and, thus, better prepare you to avoid future accidents. Now we will move to exercises to help you in a post-accident phase of a personal crisis.

Before we enter into the five principles of post-accident personal reconstruction, let us digress for just a moment. You cannot repair a problem until you know what tools you have. In other words, even before trying to reconstruct a personal incident, you should think through what your strengths are and how you can build on them.

That said, the tools that we will create are intended to guide us through our reconstruction by way of the following five cognitive actions:

1. Recognize the error
2. Accept the mistake
3. Determine whom we have hurt by having committed the error (including ourselves)
4. Seek to repair the damage done
5. Change our life course so as not to commit the error again.

In-visioning, then, is not about feelings. Feeling bad is a whole other "kettle of fish," compared to doing something about the mistake. People whom you have hurt, either on purpose or inadvertently, get very little satisfaction about the fact that you feel bad; they do, however, appreciate the fact that you have recognized your mistake and are willing to make some form of recompense. In other words, saying that you are sorry is not enough. Doing something about an error and helping to fix a problem is the way to go about reconstructing your life.

Your Positives

Most people have more strengths than they give themselves credit for. For example, are you loyal? Are you a good listener? Do you care about others? It is interesting that often people are better at listing their negatives than they are at enumerating their positives.

Exercise 3.2. Inventory your positives

Using the blank worksheet found in Appendix A.4 on page 149 or on your own sheet of paper, list your most positive traits and how they interact with your life. Figure 3.2 illustrates this exercise with a short list of four sample positives that may be your traits as well. See if you can list as many as ten.

Figure 3.2. My positives worksheet

1	I am intelligent
2	I am a good listener
3	People tend to like me
4	I am not afraid to try new things

These traits are your tools for reconstruction. Now think about how these traits can help you to go forward with your life while not neglecting to repair a past mistake.

Having positive character traits—and we all have some—is not enough. We must also recognize that we can never reconstruct a past failure by ourselves. In fact, perhaps one of the greatest myths is that of the self-made man (or woman). The reality is that from the time when we are born until the time when we die, we all need other people. Who has been important to you in your life? Whom can you count on? Who is loyal, and who is merely a temporary form of entertainment?

Your People

Developing a list of people in your life is an essential part of having the tools that you need for a successful turnaround and reconstruction. That means that you must not only know yourself, but you also have to be realistic about those with whom you interact.

Exercise 3.3. Inventory your life's people

Often, people fall into categories such as family, friends, colleagues, acquaintances, or life's passersby. Each of these groups offers us something, and some people can fall into several groups. That is to say, these groups are not mutually exclusive.

Use the blank worksheet shown in Appendix A.5 on page 150 for this exercise. Figure 3.3 provides an example of a completed worksheet.

Next to each of the five "people groups" in the left column, place the names of people who fall into each group. Once you have listed the people in your life, list the positives and the negatives of your relationships within this group. For example, you may not want to confide in a colleague at work, as too much information might either damage your career or ruin a collegial relationship. In like manner, dating a coworker may create a great deal of role confusion that will come back to haunt you at a later time.

The People Body Shop

On page 36 we reviewed the five principles of personal post-accident reconstruction and in-visioning. Our exercises are meant to help you personalize these principles. Know that this is difficult work. Looking at yourself is never easy and, just as in a gym, you need to work with these exercises daily to build the stamina needed to lift the weight of the past.

Figure 3.3. People in my life worksheet

	Name	Positive	Negative
FAMILY	Mom My sister, Misty Grandpa Charlie Aunt Emily (mom's sis)	Mom's a bit disappointed, but will support other family members (Misty and Emily always by me. And grandpa always gives good advice.	Mom is particularly critical; others more understanding. Need to be careful not to cause trouble between mom and aunt over me.
FRIENDS	Charlie (old h.s. friend) Marlene (my girl friend) Joe (music band buddy) Maria (night school friend) Steve (night school friend)	I can talk more candidly about some issues with some friends than with others, or even family, depending on the problem.	A friend today may not be a friend tomorrow. Confide only in the ones who have shown discretion in the past.
COLLEAGUES	Debbie (office assistant) Jim (work team member) Dennis (my supervisor) Amber (potential biz partner)	Friendly discussions Professional friendship Cordial friendship Is understanding	Frustrated at work as my sup. has been holding me back from promotions. Can't trust other co-workers.
ACQUAINTANCES	Harvey (neighbor) Beverly (neighbor) Paul Simon (neighbor) Amy Luz (friend)	Have an O.K. friendship with neighbors; but don't know well enough to seek their advice.	Don't know of negative issues with neighbors, but some (Paul and Beverly are neighborhood gossips.
PASSERSBY	Ben Perdun Jerry Bush (met at party) Eleanor (met at party) Marco (Joe's friend) Lynn (new classmate)	A lot in common with a few of these, but they are just people with whom I party or study.	Don't know well enough to ask for help. Except for the occasional one, they've got their own problems to worry about mine.

Exercise 3.4. Identify the damage

To begin, ask yourself the following questions about what you think your past error was:

- Was this really your error, or is it simply a cover for something far deeper?
- Are you merely scratching the surface, or have you hit pay dirt?
- Can you accept the mistake as a fact, without remorse?
- Can you forget the mistake, or that you are traumatized by it?
- Can you understand the mistake and that you are beyond the wouldas, couldas, and shouldas (see page 33)?

Now take your thoughts about these questions and formulate a description of your error or damaging act into the first line of the blank worksheet found in Appendix A.6 on page 151. See the first line of Figure 3.4 for an example of a described error. Remember that all you need to do for this exercise is complete just the first line of Appendix A.6. Having done that, you are ready to finish the form in the next exercise.

Figure 3.4. People hurt by my action worksheet

ERROR/FAULT:	DUI charge/crash into another car		
Names of People Hurt	**Direct or Indirect**	**How**	**Action To Be Taken To Fix the Problem**
Tom Smith	Directly	Medical costs and disability from my action, lost wages	I need to borrow $ to pay for costs not covered by insurance
Mom	Indirectly	She'll feel responsible	Show her that I've handled finances to pay for Tom's expenses
Grandpa Charlie	Directly	I'll need him to co-sign my loans to cover expenses	Show him I'm repaying loans on time so he won't worry

Exercise 3.5. Act to repair damage to others

Having identified the damage inflicted upon others and yourself, you are now ready for the next step: repair. Use the blank worksheet shown in Appendix A.6 on page 151 to make a list of every-one whom you have hurt by your actions, the ways in which you have hurt them, and what action you can take to fix the hurt. Figure 3.4 provides an abbreviated illustration of a completed worksheet.

An essential part of in-visioning is that you understand that saying you're sorry is not enough. You have to do something! Do not forget that there are many second- and even third-party people who may have been hurt indirectly by what you have done. You cannot repair the damage if you do not know whom you have hurt.

In-visioning is not easy. It requires a great deal of thought and attitudinal change; it entails personal interactions and per-sonal insights. The alternative, however, is a never-ending rep-etition of past accidents. If we do not wish to be like Sisyphus, rolling our past actions up a hill "for all eternity,"1 then the road to the future begins with our in-visioning in the present.

Finally, the hardest part of all: How are you going to change? What can you do to be assured that your post-action is not merely verbiage, but real actions that make you a very different person? The next exercise is intended to repair you in this way.

Exercise 3.6. Act to repair yourself

So, you now know that at some point you have messed up, made a mistake, or done something wrong. You've identified what you need to do to repair your damage to others, but what can you do for yourself to move forward?

This exercise does not ask you to complete another worksheet. Instead, we provide you with Figure 3.5, a simple checklist of points to remember and practice over time. It requires that you ingrain in yourself a new attitude and perspective on life, one step at a time, as with Lao Tzu's "thousand-mile journey" (page 11).

---

1 Sisyphus is a mythological Greek king who, for crimes that he committed against the gods, was condemned to roll a boulder uphill to the summit, only to watch it roll back down—a cycle that he was to repeat for eternity.

Figure 3.5. Attitudinal factors that affect happiness

FOURTEEN WAYS TO MAKE YOURSELF MISERABLE

We began this chapter with a quotation from Johnny Cash (page 29), who lived through many personal crises, survived them, and went on to wealth and fame. He did not have this book for advice, but he overcame his many trials and errors through actions and an attitude that are paralleled here. Let us heed his words to "build on failure"—and do the exact opposite of the following pointers from Dan Greenburg and Marcia Jacobs's (1987) book *How to Make Yourself Miserable*, lest we continue to be miserable:

1. Compare your life and accomplishments to those of other people.

2. Always look for and rely on external validation.

3. Go along with what everyone else tells you and try to please everyone.

4. Live in a sea of negative voices.

5. Spend your time looking for magic bullets that do not exist.

6. Never dare to try something new.

7. Spend your time worrying about the past and/or the future.

8. Focus on what you don't want to be or get.

9. Cling to a sense that others owe you (entitlement).

10. Make everything personal; it's all about you!

11. Focus on your problems by being self-centered.

12. Make things worse than they are.

13. Always expect the worst.

14. Just say "no thanks" to gratitude.

Although this list is offered tongue-in-cheek, it represents what many people do, even though recovery is based on the opposite actions.

In summary, to live is to err, and all of us, despite our best intentions, make mistakes, experience "crashes" in life, and have to reconstruct our lives. This chapter focused on the "after" of the event. Its theme is simple: the gates for turning your life around are always open as long as you are willing to see your mistakes, take an inventory of your life, and then decide to make the changes that are necessary.

PART

II

RECONSTRUCTION

This section discusses the four aspects of your life that need to be kept in good order, or that need to be reconstructed to achieve or regain happiness and tranquility. The four aspects, each discussed in their own chapter, are;

- Your mental health;

- Your spiritual well-being;

- The financial aspects of your life; and

- The law and you.

4

CRISES AND MENTAL HEALTH

*Everything can be taken from a man but one thing:
the last of the human freedoms—to choose one's
attitude in any given set of circumstances, to choose
one's own way.*

— Viktor Frankl

A MOTOR VEHICLE ACCOMPLISHES a simple task
using very complex means. A car gets you from point A
to point B, but to do so, it uses numerous systems that work in
unison: the braking system, the drive train, the fuel system, the
climate control system, the computer, and so on. All rely on
each other in order for the car to accomplish its simple goal. If
any one of those systems has a problem, then the least that will
happen is that you may not get where you are going. The worst
that could happen is that you could get into an accident.

These systems are interdependent and, if everything is
working correctly, they require no attention and you might not

even be aware what they are doing at any given moment. For instance, think about when you last said to yourself while driving, "I need to make sure that my fuel pump is working right now and that the alternator is producing 12.8 volts!" Probably not often, if ever, have you thought that. If something isn't working however, you lose power, you can't stop well, or it becomes really uncomfortable to drive.

When things stop working as intended, you might begin asking a lot of questions that you never thought of before about those systems and their components. After an accident, a specialist might be brought in to reconstruct the accident in order to determine what caused it. The expert might ask questions about the car such as: "Were the brakes working? Was it in good repair?" The specialist might ask about the conditions at the time of the accident, such as: "Was it raining?" Questions about the driver may also come up: "Was the driver intoxicated or tired?" The expert might even ask questions about the road, such as whether there were potholes. It is the job of this specialist to determine what contributed to the outcome, what ultimately caused the outcome, and perhaps whether driver error caused the accident or whether the accident was unavoidable because of circumstances outside of human control.

THE PARTS OF YOU

Thinking about a car is a good analogy for how individuals react in life. Personal psychology examines the ways in which we take things in from the external world around us, make sense of it, and then react through thoughts and behaviors.

Most people do not pay much attention to that process until the wheels fall off and they are forced to. Then we begin to ask questions: What caused this problem? Why am I depressed? Why am I anxious? Why can I not communicate with my spouse? Why do I get so angry? Why am I so miserable? What went wrong? Did I cause this?

It is at this point that we may find ourselves in a therapist's office, seeking consultation from a faith leader, or buying self-help books by the boxful. Maybe you find yourself scrapping the old and getting yourself a replacement; or replacing parts one at a time in an attempt to fix the problem, even though you have no real understanding of the parts. Eventually, all of your attempts to fix things end with more problems—some old, some new, but more problems, nonetheless. One thing is for sure: We are not often very good mechanics. In fact, sometimes we even make things worse.

This isn't to say that everyone needs a mental health professional. Perhaps, however, what we need are better diagnostic skills and better problem-solving skills. If you only fix symptoms, then you may ignore more important issues that are causing the problem. If you don't really know what is broken, then the chances of fixing it are not good either.

Cognitive Dissonance

In his book *Sham: How the Self-Help Movement Made America Helpless*, Steve Salerno (2005) argues convincingly that self-help products don't tend to have very long-lasting effects, and that people's psychological systems typically revert to the status quo. But why? The short answer is a phenomenon called *cognitive dissonance*.

In Aesop's fable about the fox and the grapes, the fox cannot reach some high-hanging grapes, and so he tells himself that the grapes are probably sour anyway, and therefore he does not even want them. This allows him not to be upset about being denied what he wanted.

Like the fox, when a person has desires and expectations, and those expectations are not met, only two things can happen: the person must either change their expectations ("I want the grapes, but there is just no way for me to get them, so I will have to find something else") or change his or her desire so that it matches reality and reduces anxiety about not getting what he or she wanted ("The grapes are sour, so therefore I didn't want them anyway").

People are creatures of habit, and they generally don't like to change their thinking. So it isn't much of a stretch to see that what happens most often when we get a different outcome than what we were looking for is that we come up with an explanation for the outcome, irrespective of whether the result is better or worse than what we thought we would get. Cognitive dissonance is why it is incredibly important that we examine our true, underlying needs and our expectations after there has been a crash, or to prevent a crash when we realize that we don't like the direction that we are headed in, that we aren't happy. We are good at denying our true need to fit our desires to the outcome that we got, or at explaining away a bad outcome rather than taking responsibility for it and seeing it for what it really is.

Let us look at a more specific example: Let's say that you are married or have a significant other. You have a need for love and companionship, and you expect that the relationship will continue indefinitely as long as your needs are being met. If you didn't think that, you would go into every relationship with no desire to attach because you assume that the relationship is just going to end anyway. But now, a few years in, the new has worn off, and the relationship starts to show the effects of two fallible human beings who are really getting to know each other. Conflict surfaces regarding each person's expectations that the other's behavior would stay the same indefinitely, or maybe they can no longer use cognitive dissonance to ignore unmet needs that have lingered since the beginning. Sometimes this realization happens quickly, and a quick breakup ensues. Sometimes it takes a while to surface. In any case, this is not what you expected, or your needs are just not being met!

Perhaps the reality is that you have grown disconnected

because you have taken the relationship for granted and done nothing to cultivate an environment in which the other person can feel safe and rewarded for trying to meet your needs. Maybe because it's because of what your parents taught you about relationships, or perhaps it's because your needs were catered to as a child but, in this relationship, you do nothing more than take while giving only the minimum necessary to avoid conflict.

To change the way that you act or react would require you to change your thoughts and behaviors, and that is the path of *greatest* psychological resistance. It is much easier to find a more convenient reason about why you are getting the results that you are getting. So you say: "My partner isn't nice anymore and isn't trying to make this work. This is *his* (or *her*) problem!" Perhaps you tell your spouse or partner to see a doctor, or maybe you use guilt by telling the other person, "If you loved me, you would . . ."

Perhaps you are familiar with this funny adage: "Did you know that a woman's sex drive is dependent on the food that she eats? It's true! Wedding cake kills it every time." Here, we have a perfect example of cognitive dissonance. If we believe this humorous quip, then we may conclude that the lack of sex in the marriage is, apparently, her fault and has nothing to do with the fact that her spouse expects sex without putting anything communicating and contributing to the relationship. Might the problem be that the spouse, who goes unmentioned, decided that he should not have to do anything, and that his wife should remain eternally ready to please him? This is the role of assessing desires and expectations in the context of the only thing that we can actually control—our own thoughts and behaviors.

Insight and Motivation

What is needed in situations in which expectations are not met is insight. And that very thing is often what is missing when someone reads a self-help book. Many books have good information, but without both insight and motivation, reading the good information will not help the reader to overcome a very powerful internal system that says, "Well, yes, I do those things, and that sounds like a good fix for it, but my situation is different."

We find justifications for continuing in our old beliefs or behaviors—conscious or unconscious—rather than make any lasting psychological changes. Or, often, we really do want to change things, but when we struggle, we beat ourselves up, lowering self-esteem and thereby insuring that cognitive dissonance will dominate. ("Well, I am a screw-up anyway, so what difference does it make? I am never going to be happy like other people are.")

So, if these systems are interdependent, it would sure help if we could figure out which ones present a risk for a crash or are already not functioning properly and are a proverbial accident looking for a place to happen. What we need is a way to diagnose what the problems are that have placed us on a road to a crash. We also need a way to fix them or at least reduce the danger of another crash.

Like with many things, it is always easier to prevent a crash than to deal with it once it has happened. The problem is that our motivation to think about what "might be" is low before a crash, and regret for what "we should have done" is high after a crash. So what can we do?

THE PSYCHOLOGICAL BEFORE

The way that we live our lives and the choices that we make are what lead us to where we are, and often these choices are what dictate how happy or sad we tend to be. As we will discuss in a bit, it is not the events or even the people in our lives that dictate our happiness, but rather our internal state. And that is very fortunate! It would be tragic to get to the end of your life and say, "I have had a terrible, miserable life because other people would just not do what I wanted them to do! They kept on making me unhappy and refused to do what I needed them to do in order for me to be happy."

Happiness Is a Personal Choice

Actually, our level of happiness is a matter of personal choice. Here is a definition of happiness: There is no such thing as "dark" times. That's a construct, a made-up word. There can be more or less light, but dark is just a word that we use to describe a relative lack of light. We can substitute the word "cold" for "dark." Once again, we may say that there is more or less heat and, in the case of absolute zero, no heat. Cold is just a word used to describe a relative lack of heat that is unpleasant for many of us.

Similarly, there is no such thing as happiness, but instead only a relative lack of misery. When nothing causes us misery, then we are happy. That is very different from joy, which is fleeting and very temporary. No one feels joy all the time, because it is a psychological state, not an existential state. So, if we create misery by either labeling things as miserable or by having expectations that others will "make us happy," then we are in control of our lives.

It is what you give in your life, to yourself and to others, not what others give to you, that dictates whether you are happy. There is a famous tale that Israeli farmers love to tell about Israel's three internal seas, the Hulah, the Sea of Galilee, and the Dead Sea. The Hulah gave but never took, the Galilee gives and takes, and the Dead Sea gets but does not give. The Hulah is no longer a sea, and the Dead Sea has water but no life. Only the Galilee—that which gets and gives—is teeming with life.

Give and Take

We often organize our lives, our priorities, and our relationships based on what we need and whether we feel that another person can give us what we need. It is only perhaps when we hear complaints and need to avoid discomfort that we stop to ask, "Am I capable of giving this person what he or she needs?" Couples in counseling almost invariably say some version of this: "If he would just stop doing X and start doing more of Y, then things would be better." The other party then says, "If she would just stop doing A and B all the time, then we wouldn't have any problems."

The problem with this idea as a start to getting things back on track is that, try as you might, you cannot control another human being. You can guilt people, chide them, humiliate them, beg, plead, etc., but if how you want them to behave isn't a good match with who they are, the results are probably not going to impress you. So, what do you have control over? Well, yourself, of course! You can focus on being your version of a good spouse.

THE PSYCHOLOGICAL AFTER

After a crash has occurred, things can get messier still. The sudden realization hits that there was a problem, and the next question is, "How could this have happened?" or "Why me?"

Inevitably, the self-talk that a person engages in after a crash has two themes. You either blame yourself or others, or a combination of the two. If either reaction is used exclusively, it probably isn't healthy. The easiest path is of course to blame others, which allows you to avoid responsibility and thereby avoid painful self-blame and guilt for a mistake that you made. By doing so, however, you do not learn from the mistake, and the accident that it caused is never reconstructed and examined accurately, so no one gets closure.

When you fail to see your part in what happened and fail to make the appropriate changes to prevent it from happening again, then recovery is not possible and the probability of making the same mistake over and over again is high. Looking at another's fault without examining your fault, or even outright blaming others for your mistakes, can also cause more damage after the wreck, because your punishing others alienates them and increases the likelihood of another wreck.

However, you may be right. Maybe others really did cause the problem. But if you are determined to place blame on others and to be angry about their actions, then ask yourself whether you are choosing to be miserable and open to being hurt by others.

The bottom line is this: We can never control other people's behavior. Pointing out to them that they have wronged you gives you no more ability to make them act differently, and thus you are just as powerless after you blame them than you were before.

What You Can Control

The one thing that you *do* have control over is *you*. You have control over whom you choose to associate with, what situations you allow yourself to get into, how vulnerable you make yourself, and how you react, emotionally and psychologically, to other people's behaviors. That is the only thing that you have control over—yourself. Now, take a few minutes for the following two mental exercises that help exemplify this point.

Exercise 4.1. List the hurts that others have caused you

In this mental exercise, think of as many as three things that others have said to you or did that you perceived as negative. Then consider the following questions to understand how you reacted:

- What possible actions would you take in response to these hurts?
- Which aspects of these situations could you control?
- What were the advantages of the way that you reacted?
- What were the disadvantages of the way that you reacted?
- When the situation has come to its termination, what would you like to feel?

If you decided that blaming yourself is more appropriate, then remember that the problem with self-blame is that it is usually exaggerated and irrational. The purpose of beating yourself up is to "punish" yourself somehow so that you won't make that mistake again.

When you punish yourself, you doubt your own ability to self-regulate, you feel worse about yourself, and you can become so engrossed in wallowing in self-blame and self-pity that you can't focus on what needs to happen next. It's about self-blame and not about objectively assessing what happened and what you need to do from this point to get out of this situation and not look back.

Exercise 4.2. List what you did wrong and regret

In this mental exercise, think of what you know that you did wrong and now regret. How did you handle these regrets? From the following examples, which might you choose as your reaction? What other options might you choose?

- Apologize to the person.
- Ask what you can do to fix it.
- Seek psychological help.
- Forget about the mistake.
- Analyze your mistake and find a way not to repeat it.
- Punish yourself for life.
- Punish others for your mistake.
- Discuss each of these possibilities with a friend or colleague.

With self-blame, the key element is always guilt. We often use guilt as a tool. We tell ourselves that we should feel guilty because it feels right emotionally to beat ourselves up. Just as children fundamentally and intrinsically look for discipline from a parent, adults seek a way to do penitence for past mistakes and to find a way to recover from these past errors.

About Guilt

Psychologically speaking, there is more than one form of guilt. For example, people can suffer from useful guilt and/or non-useful guilt. Let's assume that you have stolen a car. A balanced person will then feel some form of guilt for having broken the law or having intentionally hurt another person.

Useful guilt forms the checks-and-balances system that is built into most human beings who live by a standard moral code. Although the moral code is different for different cultures, all cultures have a moral code. Useful guilt forces us to view our lives from within the perspective of the "We" rather than merely from the perspective of the "I."

Nonuseful guilt has nothing to do with a moral code, but is rather based on the need to punish. We sometimes feel guilt only because people around us or our cultural customs tell us that we should.

An interesting subcategory of nonuseful guilt is *manipulative guilt,* which occurs when others say that they are sorry so that they are relieved of any responsibility. In this case, the apology acts as a conduit for transferring the guilt from the perpetrator to the victim.

Such nonuseful guilt serves no purpose other than to punish, and it is useless in bringing real change or helping you to recognize more-appropriate behaviors. It only punishes. Sure, you might seek to avoid more punishment and not engage in the behavior again but, more likely, you'll get used to the punishment and learn to incorporate it into who you are and how you think. You might get to the point that you punish yourself with guilt for literally everything, because it becomes habit.

Internal Stockholm syndrome, another form of nonuseful guilt, resembles actual Stockholm syndrome. With internal Stockholm syndrome, we develop sympathy with the part of ourselves that gets beaten up when we blame ourselves. We learn to be comfortable with guilt and blame, and will even miss it terribly if we no longer have it.

An unfortunate part of this psychological mechanism is exemplified in the following true tale from the early life of this chapter's author, Tom Marrs:

A DOG'S TALE

I grew up in a junkyard. Growing up, we always had stray animals hanging around the place. Once, we had a stray dog that befriended the men who worked in the yard. For perverse entertainment, one of them placed a large metal gasket over the dog's head and fashioned it as a collar.

The dog tried for days to get the gasket off. After about a month of wearing this cumbersome thing, my grandmother felt sorry for the dog and pulled the gasket off from around her neck.

We then watched as the dog ran her nose back in the same hole in the gasket as my grandmother held it, and forced her head back in. She tried to throw it away, but the dog was ill at ease and felt as though something was missing. The dog retrieved it and tried to get it back on.

Why did the dog behave this way? For the same reason that people continue with behaviors that are not healthy and bring them pain. It becomes comfortable and brings psychological security.

To break old habits, to change behaviors, we must endure being without our psychological security blankets. Many people would prefer to avoid change rather than discontinue their unhealthy behaviors. So, in light of the dog's tale, ask yourself these questions: Does change bother you? If so, why? How can you motivate yourself to change?

Expectations Are in the Mind

Every human being experiences some stress associated with change. The *pain-pleasure principle* dictates that we do more of what feels good, and less of what feels bad (Laplanche and Pontalis, 1988). People often go through a "crisis of change" when things suddenly feel unsure and we feel out of control or like we aren't sure of what to expect.

It might be said that expectations are the root of much of what causes crashes in peoples' lives. People expect to get different results from the same behavior, or expect to get what they have always gotten, even when conditions or circumstances change. The "Gremlin" automobile in the sidebar below illustrates this.

EXPECTATIONS CAN HAVE GREMLINS

If you go to your car, put the key in the ignition, and turn it, what do you expect to happen? You probably expect it to start. In fact, if it does, you won't even think twice about it, much less even pay attention to the fact that it started. But if you turn the ignition and get the telltale clicking of a dead battery, how do you feel? Stressed? Will you be late? Is it the battery? The alternator? How much will this cost? How will I get there? But is it the car not starting that is really causing the problem?

Let's modify the situation to see if we can get a different reaction to the same event. What if you drive a 1974 AMC Gremlin, and it breaks down all the time. It runs sometimes, but you are always having problems with it. If you put the key in the ignition, turn it, and get nothing, are you as stressed? Probably not. You are used to having problems with the car, and thus your expectations are different. So, this means that the event—the result—is not where the problem lies, but is instead the psychological adherence to an expectation.

In fact, no event has *any* meaning. The meaning comes from what you think about the event, not some inherent meaning that is associated with the event. If you have a wreck, then is it horrible and terrible? As Eckert Tolle (2008) put it in his book *A New Earth*, things are "horrible" and "terrible" because you say that they are "horrible" and "terrible"—not because the event has any inherent meaning. Change what you say, and you will change its psychological meaning and the impact that it has.

Exercise 4.3. View events from a different perspective

For this exercise, start by listing three things in your head that you do not like in your life, then consider the following questions:

- How have you described, or viewed, these things in the past?
- Going forward, what might be a better way to describe them?

This simple exercise may help you to reorganize your thinking so that you have a more positive outlook on life, one that should lead to greater happiness.

Roles That Define Us

Part of the reason that we have expectations is that we like to play roles. In other words, we like to define ourselves so that we can neatly put a label on who we are. We don't do very well if we can't fit ourselves and others into neat categories like "jerk," or "sweet."

The problem is that once we define ourselves, we start playing that role, and we try hard to maintain the behavior that supports the roles that we define ourselves by. If you see yourself as a "nice guy," then you need to maintain behaviors all the time that support that role. If you deviate and say "no" to someone who wants your help, then you are not meeting the obligations and expectations of the role—the sense of self—that you have previously been rewarded for playing.

Guilt feels bad. So when we tell ourselves a story that produces guilt, it is very natural to be drawn back to a familiar behavior that reduces the guilt, even if it means causing more problems. For example, when you feel overloaded and stressed, you might recognize that you have to learn to say no to requests for your time. But then you may have guilt that feels even worse than the stress, so you might agree to take on more work and projects, until you are so overloaded that you have a nervous breakdown. That results in a crash.

The problem with role-playing is that it does not account for the full range of human behavior. Would you consider yourself to be a good person? Probably so. Have you ever been mean to another person? Have you ever taken something that wasn't yours—a pen or pencil from work, perhaps? Then how can you say that you are a good person, since aren't the behaviors of a good person? Labels are black or white, and being a human being is *not* a black or white issue. There is a wide range of human behavior.

One of the roles that people are good at playing, and one that certainly carries with it many expectations, involves our roles in religion. If we tell ourselves or others, "I am a good Christian," for instance, and then our humanness inevitably comes out, and we act in ways that are counter to the definition of a good Christian, then we feel guilty. We tell ourselves that we are frauds and have let everyone, including God, down. This is nonuseful guilt because often it distracts us from understanding our behavior and preventing it from happening in the future. The guilt lowers self-esteem and prevents the development of wisdom about how to handle the situations that human beings get themselves into.

Because very black-or-white rules often accompany roles, we get into playing those roles because having things be black or white reduces our anxiety about ambiguity. But with either-or situations, there is no room for useful ambiguity. For example, when we go to a member of the clergy, a psychologist, an educator, or a lawyer for help, what are we really attempting to get? Answers. And why would you go to another person for answers? Because he or she specializes in giving direction, by the nature of what he or she does. They help us to clarify what we have not succeeded in clarifying for ourselves and thus reduce our anxiety by giving direction to our lives.

Direction is difficult to find, though, if you are fighting the programmed roles that you play that result from your family, your community, your culture. The only aspect about learned behaviors that is ultimately "bad" is when those learned behaviors result in misery because they either fail to get us what we do want or because they result in our getting something that we know we do *not* want.

In most cases, there is no inherent good or bad cultural teaching. The issue with learned behavior is that it is most often so unconsciously held that we don't recognize it as the source of the decision-making that has led us to a crash.

What decisions have you made that were costly to you emotionally, financially, legally, or spiritually that you made without thought or purpose? Was it actually because of habit or desire not to break with "who you are"? There is an old saying that applies here: sometimes the devil you know is better than the angel you have yet to meet.

Ultimately, if we have little flexibility in our behavior, and we fail to learn why we crashed and how not to crash in the future, then we are destined to repeat mistakes and cause ourselves a lot of misery in life.

Self-Awareness and Validation

If we invest much time and energy in protecting our sense of self and, in the process, others fail to recognize or validate those behaviors, then it is upsetting to us as well. If I am a "good person," then do I feel entitled to be treated as such by all those around me? And do I feel angry or slighted if others fail to see me in the way that I wish to be seen? How many times have we heard or maybe said, "I am a good person! What did I do to deserve this? Why does God hate me? Why don't people like me? Why can't I get a break in life?" In that moment of self-pity, there is a lack of awareness or acknowledgement of *our* responsibility in what got us there.

Self-awareness and ego are characteristics that are entirely unique to human beings. To quote D. H. Lawrence's (1930) "Self-Pity" poem, "I have never seen a wild thing feel sorry for itself. A little bird will fall dead, frozen from a bough, without ever having felt sorry for itself." We constantly compare our view of our self and our behaviors with what others do and say in an act of validation, a feeling of belonging, and competition with others to feel justified in our existence.

Either way, we have an emotional investment in making sure that what we get matches with what we think we deserve, rather than looking at the simple statement, "Have my decisions moved me closer to where I want to be? And, what can I control, compared to what I have no control over?"

The only way to get away from that pattern is by using consciousness—presence in the here and now—to assess the situation, figure out what went wrong or what might go wrong, and determine the best course of action, knowing that you will undoubtedly have to make corrections along the way.

Anger Is Passing

Finally, the one emotion above all others that contributes to a crash is anger. So far, we have not effectively addressed the anger that everyone feels occasionally. How many times has anger—and have the resulting decisions that we make when we feel it—led us to make a crash worse, involve innocent bystanders, or even further injure ourselves?

If what we have discussed so far were a complete answer about how to prevent a crash, then you would simply look at the situation, determine whether something could be done, or—if you have no ability to change it—rationalize the situation. And with that, there would never be a need for anger. But that isn't the reality of being a human being. All people feel anger from time to time, regardless of whether it is rational to do so, and irrespective of whether we could "choose" to feel something else. When you are wronged, when you are a victim, or when others cause you pain, anger is a normal reaction.

Rather than try to talk you out of feeling anger by warning you of the potential consequences, let's look at how to handle it when you inevitably *do* feel anger so that you can deal with the anger rather than cause a crash. We'll start by looking at how you react to anger.

Exercise 4.4. Examine how you react to anger

This exercise should help you to recognize whether you are predisposed to angry outbursts or negative reactions that may cause a crash, rather than to dealing with situations in ways that minimize the damage to you. Conversely, you may discover that you generally handle stress and disappointment well.

Using the blank worksheet shown in Appendix A.7 on page 152, list the last three times when your anger was seriously triggered by someone or something. Remember that we experience some level of anger daily or almost daily, but these are not always significant events.

Next, enter into the worksheet how you responded and what the outcome of the incident was either during or immediately after the episode.

The purpose of the exercise is to help you gauge your temperament. Do this by adding up each column. If you score a three (3) in the "better" or "worse" column, then that probably means that your responses to stress tend either to mitigate or inflame stressful situations, and you likely believe that your responses soothe you or leave you stressed. See Figure 4.1 for an example of a completed exercise.

Anger in and of itself doesn't cause problems. However, if we make decisions while we are angry, then—like trying to steer the car while we are in emotional turmoil—bad things ensue. The best thing that you can do when you feel angry is at least to have a contract with yourself not to act while you are in the throes of anger.

Figure 4.1. How I deal with anger worksheet

Anger Trigger (What Made You Mad?)	Your Response	The Situational Outcome			Your Emotional Outcome		
		Better	Same	Worse	Better	Same	Worse
Boss reprimanded me for late work (that was late because Jim didn't get the spreadsheet done)	I tried to reason that it wasn't my fault. He said I was in charge. I threatened to quit.		X		X		
Mary Ann (spouse) screamed at me for 2nd late car payment (may result in lower credit score)	I first tried to explain I didn't have time to handle home budget, then screamed at her when she argued back		X				X
Another driver cut me off on a highway and flicked me off	chased after him and got into a screaming match. Almost got into a roadside fight		X				X
TOTALS			3		1		2

Remember that this is only a "quick-and-dirty" exercise and not a true psychological/personality test. It is for your own use as a way to begin to articulate and understand yourself and your behavior.

INSTRUCTIONS:
1. List the **last** three instances you remember in which you were seriously angered by someone or something (e.g., getting reprimanded at work or school, a loud argument with your spouse/friend, etc.)
2. Enter how you responded (e.g., tried to reason, insulted back, threw something, etc.)
3. Check an option in the situational block to indicate what the outcome to your response was.
4. Check an option in the emotional block to indicate how you felt about it after your response.
5. Total each column to see what your behavior tends to be in anger-inducing situations.

SITUATIONAL DIAGNOSTIC (people generally interpret the results in the following fashion):
3 Better outcomes = You believe your responses work for you in defusing stressful situations.
3 Worse outcomes = You recognize your responses are inflammatory to stressful situations.

EMOTIONAL DIAGNOSTIC (people generally interpret the results in the following fashion):
3 Better outcomes = Your responses generally alleviate your stress (they work for you).
3 Worse outcomes = Your responses are self-injurious (they hurt your emotional well-being).

Responses in-between (usually 2's) are "trending" to the response category where most points are.

Think about a time when you had an argument or fight with a spouse or family member. As each of you became more and more angry, at the end of the argument, did you actually work through anything? Was any resolution really gained? Often, nothing is resolved, because we cannot think rationally while angry. Physiologically, we are set up to react to anger by becoming really focused on the thing that caused the anger. How can you make good choices if you can't look effectively at the situation?

You might find that you are angry a lot. Do you have a hair trigger on your anger mechanism? The more stress that we get under, the lighter the trigger becomes. At some point, it is no longer about the anger—no longer the case that what you say makes you angry. It is about going through life feeling justified to be angry. When you feel justified, you focus on holding on to your anger because it feels right and deserved, and so you feel as though you should not set it down. Often, you victimize yourself much worse than the anger-provoking incident did, because you then go through life angry and upset for a much longer period of your life than you needed to. To what end do you maintain the "rightness" of your anger, then?

When you do feel anger, it is okay to allow yourself that guilty pleasure. Sometimes, you just want to be angry and don't want to be talked out of it. But don't add real damage to anger by making decisions or acting while you are angry. Have you ever been mad at a friend for something that he or she did? Are you as angry today as you were when it happened? What about five years from now? Will you be as angry? If the answer is no, then realize that anger passes, and with it the desire to act out of anger. Looking back, do you feel like you could make better decisions about how to handle the situation now, today, than you did at the time when it happened?

Saying it now makes sense and is rational, but when you are angry you feel very justified to be angry and, therefore, to act in response. The thought that you have to frame in your mind is that you may be justified, and the target of your anger may deserve a specific consequence; but if that is true, will you not feel that way tomorrow as well? Would you not feel that way in a week?

So, we can summarize this section on anger by examining the different kinds of anger that you may experience:

Healthy anger allows us to learn from our mistakes and to be a better judge of people through a desire to avoid the misery of being angry.

Unhealthy anger is anger that we indulge in the same way that we indulge in too much in our favorite food. It tastes good now, but if you don't make a conscious decision to stop at some point, you will pay for it later.

■ ■ ■

In summary, psychological factors that contribute to our life-altering crashes are rarely things that other people create in us, rarely things we have no control over, and often very difficult to spot through self-examination alone.

It often takes either an outside person who can see the bigger picture or, more often, our ability to recognize the warning signs of a crash, and the desire and ability to change the direction in which you are headed. If you get in a car wreck because of your habit of following too closely—and you find it too difficult to break the habit, so you continue to follow too closely—are you not destined to get into another wreck? If someone taps his brakes to alert you to how close you are, and you don't make a decision to back off, are you not then eventually going to suffer from your inability to change unsafe conditions?

A good way to start avoiding personal crashes is to recognize that many of your troubles emanate from poorly controlled emotions, and then actively work to understand and control them in the following ways:

1. Recognize cognitive dissonance in yourself—the inability to match your expectations successfully to reality—and instead seek cognitive "harmony" by adjusting your expectations.

2. Understand that happiness is within you, in your mindset— how you choose to define your environment in relative terms like good and bad, beautiful and ugly, hot and cold, wonderful and terrible, and so on. Choose to see things in a better light rather than in a worse light.

3. Accept that control is mostly within you. You can control yourself and your actions, but rarely can you control others or their actions.

4. Finally, learn to not act when you find yourself in the inevitable grip of the most troublesome emotion of all: anger. Train yourself to wait for anger to pass. Refrain from acting or making rash decisions while angry. Anger is the one emotion that causes the greatest number of crashes.

CHAPTER

5

SPIRITUAL WELLNESS

*Religion is for those who don't want to go to hell,
and spirituality is for those who have already been
there.*

— Elizabeth Gilbert
"Eat, Pray, Love"

THERE IS NO doubt that spirituality is difficult to define. For example, you can go to the Internet to determine your spirituality type. Some websites such as Belief-O-Matic (n.d.) can even score your spiritual type. Although it is impossible to reduce a person's spirituality to a computerized number (there are too many variables and degrees), it is important to ask questions like these: What is my place in the universe? What is the meaning of my life? How do I make moral decisions? Are we merely intelligent animals, or do we exist for a purpose beyond ourselves?

How we react to these questions determines a great deal

about our life choices. We may, for instance, ask ourselves about whether we have children merely because of a biological necessity or whether we bring children into the world for a deeper, more spiritual reason. Is it moral to bring children into a world of suffering, or do we believe that human beings may not have all the answers? Are we the center of our worlds, or do we exist for a purpose beyond ourselves?

A DEFINITION OF SPIRITUALITY

From the most pious followers of a faith to the most committed atheists (and everything in between), what makes us human is our cognitive ability to ponder our existence and place in the universe. René Descartes' (1987) famous philosophical dictum—*cogito, ergo sum* ("I think, therefore I am")—comes to mind in this regard.

We may hold a clear vision of our God (or Gods, in some cultures) or question the notion that humanity should even pretend to understand the universe or the existence of a supreme being. But regardless, the question of our purpose on earth intrudes into all our minds.

As we mentioned in the introduction (see "On God and Personal Reconstruction" on page xv), you should take our references to God to mean your notion of who or what God is. Our purpose is to help you achieve spiritual wellness through what we believe are universal tenets for humanity.

Our purpose is to shine a light on the path from spiritual despair—a void of relationships and meaning—to spiritual tranquility—a state of relative peace with yourself and those who surround you in life, a tranquility that is achieved through the practice of the "Key Principles of Reconstructive Spirituality" on page 78 that we will encourage you to adopt and practice going forward.

A better definition of spirituality will become evident to you as you read through this chapter and perform the exercises.

PRACTICING SPIRITUALITY

Spirituality goes from obligation to opportunity. For example, in his book, *Conversations with God*, Donald Neale Walsch (1999, 377) writes:

> Opportunity, not obligation, is the cornerstone of religion, the basis of all spirituality. So long as you see it the other way around, you will have missed the point. Relationship—your relationship to all things—was created as your perfect tool in the work of the soul. That is why all human relationships are sacred ground. It is why every personal relationship is holy.

These are fascinating words. Do you agree that relationships are opportunities rather than obligations? Is this the reason that men often back off when a woman states that she has "invested" a number of years in a relationship? Are relationships windows into the depths of our souls? If so, what do you see through your window?

Think about the impact of your spiritual assumptions regarding the way that you do business and handle money. Or, regarding the law, do you have the sense that the world was created only for your sake? Do laws exist only for others or for those who are too stupid to learn how to get around them? Are you passionate about your work, family, friends, and significant other? Do you see work and food as only a means to survive, or do you relish life and get the most out of each day?

Most religions have a word for breaking their laws: *sin*. Biblical Hebrew, however, does not see sin as a transgression against God but rather as a lost opportunity. The Hebrew verb *to sin* means "to miss the mark," or "to lose an opportunity." As such, is the greatest sin of all the misuse of a day? Think of the many ways that you misuse the gift of time. How have you missed your mark because of false pride or by alienating yourself from others?

Exercise 5.1. Discover how to use your time wisely

Use the blank worksheet shown in Appendix A.8 on page 155 to list as many as five ways that you have "missed the mark" and how these missed marks have negatively impacted your life. Figure 5.1 provides an abbreviated illustration of this exercise.

Figure 5.1. Using my time wisely worksheet

Your "Sin" (Missed Mark)	Negative Life Impact
Got drunk at a party and missed work	Chastised by my supervisor and told I could be fired next time I miss work, beat myself up for being stupid, and lost 8 hours of wages.
Got in an argument with a man at the grocery store about politics	It ate up 10 minutes I can't get back, I was upset and distracted for 2 hours afterward thinking of things I could have said to him, and feel bothered I couldn't get him to see the error in his thinking.
I spent 8 hours looking at profiles on a dating website this weekend	I started a lot of conversations with people who were interesting....but not people I really care to date. I feel even more distracted and confused about my options now.

This chapter will not solve all of your spiritual dilemmas. We do not seek here to defend or defile religion, or to justify any one particular faith or religious system. Instead, this chapter seeks to help you deepen your individual growth as a person. Its goal is to help you to find your path in the universe and to understand your own personal *raison d'être* ("reason for existence").

It is essential here to emphasize that this chapter about spirituality is not a substitute for psychological help or a psychologist. Psychology is all about our problems in "living." Among the many things that psychology does is to address our fears, compulsions, and unresolved past issues.

This chapter takes a different route. It looks at our relationship to whatever or whomever we define as God or where we fit into a world that is greater than any of us or of all of us.

The classical Jewish morning prayer says it best: It is not our job merely to find ourselves. Rather, it is our job to understand, to discern, to perceive, to learn, and to teach through example. Spirituality is more about doing something—in the sense of "to *do* life"—than it is about feeling.

Spirituality, then, addresses the full range of issues, from fear to ethics, from war to relationships with others and with God. Spirituality is the sense that even when you are by yourself, you are not alone, and that aloneness does not mean loneliness.

Prayer

There are many ways to spirituality. One way is through prayer. Most religions have several forms of prayer. Sociologically speaking, prayer may be formal (that is, set by a specific ritual), and informal (such as with spontaneous prayer), and it can take place in private or in public settings.

Prayer is not an easy word to describe. It is not a magic formula but, rather, a way to see the world more clearly, a positioning of oneself within the context of a universe that is composed of both time and space. It can help you during a time of rebuilding by providing an opportunity to hear your desires and contemplate them, and have the most difficult of dialogues—the one that is internal and honest and within yourself.

Work

Another way that we express our spirituality is through work. Work in the scriptures is not a dirty word; it is not something to be avoided. Rather, work is a way to define our humanity. Work is not punishment but the chance to explore our creativity. Note that many religions not only command to rest on the seventh day but also to work on the other six days of the week.

Work can be viewed as a form of prayer. It can be nothing more than a way to earn one's keep, or it can be used to take us to a greater meaning, to become "fixers of the world"—that is, to make the world a better place. Not only do we work to earn money, but also the spiritual person works toward self-improvement. To work, to struggle with oneself, is a form of prayer. It is the essence of defining who we are and what we are about.

Work symbolizes that no one in this world owes us anything, that God has given us capabilities and opportunities, and that it is up to us to use them or to lose them. The spiritual person knows that the choice is his or hers.

DEVELOPING LISTENING SKILLS

Spirituality's number-one tool is listening. The old adage that "seeing is believing" is a lot less true than is "life is about hearing and responding." To hear means to listen to our inner voice. Listening is our most important tool during times of crisis.

After a crisis has come to its conclusion, often we hear people remark that they knew all along that they were going down the wrong path. The inner self was speaking to them, but they chose not to hear it. Personal crises are often not about what happens to us externally but rather what happens to us internally. That means that we need not only to listen to ourselves, but also to have the inner discipline necessary to take the time to hear what we know to be true.

Exercise 5.2. Assess your listening skills
Listening does not come easily. Human beings are adept at both hearing and choosing not to hear. In developing your spiritual hearing skills, think about what prevents you from listening.

Use the blank worksheet shown in Appendix A.9 on page 154 to see how well you can honestly fill in the blanks. Figure 5.2 provides an example of a completed worksheet.

Figure 5.2. Assess your listening skills worksheet

Obstacle	What Stops You
Too much noise in our lives	No problem here. I can tune out noise.
Fear of quiet	No problem here either.
Too busy to hear	I'm usually too much in a hurry to stop to think through problems and shoot from the hip
Impatience	Also, don't want to devote too much time to things
Fear of change	I don't know if this is a problem.
Fear of being unworthy	I don't like for people to think that I can't solve problems on my own, so I go my way and not what others suggest.
Fear of the answer	Too many people criticize the way I do things. I want my solutions to be the right way.

THINGS THAT HOLD US BACK FROM SPIRITUALITY

There are at least two characteristics, or emotions, that have a great effect on our lives and hold us back from spirituality. Let's examine them and see whether these are traits that have affected you.

Egocentricity is perhaps the first thing that holds us back from a sense of spirituality. The Hebrew word for "secular" is derived from the word that means "hollow" or "void." Highly egocentric people see the world as revolving around them. Because they are the center of their world, there is no room for others to enter it and no place for laws outside of themselves to guide them, and they often equate money with power.

We have no exercise for this condition and, unfortunately, egocentrics are unlikely to recognize themselves as such. Why should they? The world owes them, or so they think and act. But those who do recognize this trait in themselves may want to work on this, perhaps under the guidance of a psychologist. It is to their benefit in order to achieve spirituality.

Fear is another intangible that holds us back. How many of us suffer from a multitude of fears that control our lives? The non-spiritual person often fears what others may say, change, and what the future may bring. These, however, are not our only fears. What other fears do you have?

Exercise 5.3. Identify the fears that diminish your life
Use the blank worksheet shown in Appendix A.10 on page 157 to note not only your fears, but also how these fears diminish the quality of your life and the lives of others with whom you interact. Figure 5.3 provides an illustration of this exercise.

MONEY AND SPIRITUALITY

Perhaps nothing undercuts our sense of spirituality more than do issues of finance. As noted in chapter 1, how we handle money teaches us a great deal about who we are and what we represent. Money is not evil. What we do with money can be good or evil, helpful or hurtful.

The spiritual person is not afraid of wealth but seeks wealth to appreciate life more, rather than to make himself or herself into a demigod. The spiritual person does not seek money in order to symbolize worthiness but rather as part of his or her responsibility to grow and to help others to grow. The money-oriented

person is consumed with envy and jealousy; the spiritually oriented person sees money as merely one more tool with which to play in the game of life.

Figure 5.3. Fears that diminish my life worksheet

My Fear	How It Diminishes My Life
Public speaking	I'm really good at my work and have been asked to do presentations but I turn them down and I lose work opportunities as a result
Driving on highways	I'm scared to even change lanes because of zooming traffic and I miss exits, and I rely too much on others to drive me if highway driving is involved
My kids won't turn out how I hope	It makes me controlling at times and drives my family nuts, and I make decisions about what is best only for the kids and not me.
I will never find a person who loves me for who I am	I don't always let my true self show around others. I stay in bad relationships too long, and worry more about if they like me than if I really like them.
I can never be truly happy	I don't allow myself to enjoy little things that make me happy because I think things will turn out badly.

Charity can take the form of time or money. When we give our time, we give of ourselves. In many ways, time is worth more than money. There are things that money just can't buy. Giving our time—ourselves—for others, particularly those in need or grief, is a kind of giving that can be priceless. However, having money is what allows us to be financially charitable.

Charity is not merely what we choose to give to others; it is a way that we make others and ourselves right and permits us to interact with our community and our world. Charity connects us with people beyond our immediate circle who are most in need of our reach.

Figure 5.4. How I use money worksheet

Main Monetary Expenses	What These Expenses Symbolize
Mortgage	A home for my family. Rest and shelter.
Groceries	Health for my family. Abundance.
Charity donations	Relief for the hungry, less advantaged. A shelter for homeless kids. Sympathy.

Exercise 5.4. Examine how you use your money

Use the blank worksheet shown in Appendix A.11 on page 156 to examine your spending habits. What do your money management practices say about who you are and what you stand for? Figure 5.4 illustrates some types of expenses that you may also have. Your list should be longer than the list in the example.

SPIRITUALITY AND BEING PART OF THE COMMUNITY

Despite the mistaken belief that being spiritual means being alone, the meaning of true spirituality is far from a withdrawal from the world. Very much to the contrary, a spiritual person interacts with this world and seeks to improve it by means of his presence.

To be a truly spiritual person, you have to interact not only with your concept of God, but also with those who surround you. Spiritual people seek to become God's helpers in repairing the world, in clothing the naked, in feeding the hungry, and in comforting the bereaved.

The spiritual person gives charity not because he or she has to, but rather because it is the right thing to do. It is not merely about giving money. It is also about interacting with others.

Take the time now to review your life. How have you given of yourself or wealth? Are you generous or selfish with your time? Do you help others or merely take from them? How you answer these questions will tell you as much about your sense of spirituality as it does about your belief system.

In the end, spirituality is not about believing; rather, it is about doing.

■ ■ ■

In summary, there are several key points to consider in your quest for spiritual wellness:

1. Use your time wisely. Your time and life are limited. Even those of us who are in a "purgatory" of sorts (e.g., incarceration, or prolonged restrictions because of illness or injury) can turn our minds to self-reconstructive activities. This can be in the service of others or in preparation for your invisioned life.

2. Learn to listen, or improve your listening skills. True listening is both difficult and the most important tool of self-reconstruction. Listen to your own inner voice and really listen to others.

3. Face your fears. We all have them. Find ways to overcome fears or to sidestep the ones that you can't. Most of all, avoid being self-centered.

4. Use money for good, helpful purposes. The pursuit of money consumes the person with envy and jealousy. Money is merely a tool for a better life for your family, yourself, and others in need or grief. But remember also that time can be more valuable than money. Generously give your time to others.

Finally, we offer the following thirteen key principles of reconstructive spirituality. You may already be practicing some or most of them. Continue in your quest toward spiritual wellness by adopting and practicing as many of them as possible.

KEY PRINCIPLES OF RECONSTRUCTIVE SPIRITUALITY

Many a book has been written on spirituality, but our method is to speak less and to do more. In order to help you realize spirituality, that is, live it, here are a number of principles to guide you. Try to connect each one with the other aspects of this book, the legal, the financial and the psychological.

1. Rather than saying your sorry, do not do it.

2. Faith is meaningless if you do not practice it.

3. Wisdom does not come with an expiration date.

4. What we do and what we say reflect who we are.

5. Money is neither evil nor good, it is merely a tool to help us in life.

6. Relationships are the building blocks of happiness. Seek relationships with yourself, with your colleagues, with your friends, with your family and with God.

7. Do something nice every day.

8. Be charitable with your time and money.

9. Take time out to think. You are worth very little to others if you do not take care of yourself.

10. Remember that you are not the center of the universe. Interaction with others is the key to good living.

11. Work allows the creative juices to flow and gives us a framework in which to live.

12. Each stage in life has its own blessings. Do not regret what you did or did not do in the past, but rather work hard to make the future a better place.

13. Life is composed of units of time. Do not waste time, but rather make every moment of life a gift from God.

C H A P T E R

6

ESSENTIAL PERSONAL FINANCES

If you haven't figured it out yet, an absolutely
certain way to lose something as quickly as
possible is to forget the privilege you have to
possess it in the first place.

— Craig Lounsbrough

IN THE BROADWAY musical *Cabaret*, we hear the song "Money Makes the World Go Round." Money is an essential part of life. Without it, we soon lose control over our lives. Money may not buy love, but it does buy food and shelter, and it permits us to prioritize our lives and organize our needs.

Personal finance is the way that we organize and use our money. It is the way that we manage our resources, acquire new resources, and watch over the money that we have. The financial component of life is the least difficult to identify and often the most difficult to solve. Finances create personal crashes, and financial solutions are often difficult to in-vision.

IN-VISIONING FOR FINANCE

There are several general principles to follow in order to improve or correct your finances when in-visioning.

Always pay on time. Never count on next month's earnings. Perhaps the biggest mistake that we can make is to count on money that we do have. Things happen, people do not pay, and you can never tell a creditor that not paying a bill is someone else's fault.

Learn about the world of finance. Knowledge is power and, in the world of finances, ignorance can be deadly. Learn the basic terms of finance, understand your bank statement, and take the time to read what is written in small print. Live within your means, because debt is costly. The best way not to lose money is to avoid debt. Before using a credit card, consider whether you really need the item at hand. Credit card companies do more than charge interest; they often charge usurious amounts.

Watch your money. Know where your money is, what you are receiving for your money, and how to distinguish between the real message about what you want to purchase from a marketing ploy. You are the only one who is responsible for your finances. It is amazing how many people have money in bank accounts about which they have forgotten. Consider why you are purchasing a specific item before you do so. Do you tend to buy things that you cannot afford so as to impress others?

Establish clear and concrete financial goals. Even youngsters can establish clear goals. Younger people can afford higher levels of risk; older people need to be more prudent. Remember that our acceptable level of risk depends on age and circumstance. A healthy, single man who is around forty years of age can take more risks than can a sickly, single grandfather.

Know how to save. For example, do not buy a car that you cannot afford. If you cannot afford a new car, then keep the one that you already have for a longer time and schedule regular maintenance. On the whole, leasing a vehicle is not a smart idea. It is better to have less and own it than to have more and give it all up at the end of a few years. In like manner, especially in a time of rising food prices, eat in, not out, and take your lunch to work rather than eat at a restaurant. Finally, remember that smoking not only hurts your health, but also your pocketbook. Smoking literally "burns up your money." Kick the habit and save!

ADOLESCENTS AND FINANCES

Adolescents are special people. They often seek to discover their own identity because they are unsure of who they are. Frequently, they are disconnected from reality.

Many adolescents are confused about the value of money. Although all of us may suffer from keeping-up-with-the-Joneses syndrome, it is especially common among teenagers. Some teenagers judge themselves not on who they are but by what they have or wear. This can lead them to value money mistakenly as the means necessary for expressing their identity.

Before the Crisis

The social norms of adolescents may manifest themselves as multiple problems that lead to a personal crash. For example, because many teenagers see money in highly symbolic terms, they may place unfair demands on their parents. And parents often feel that they are held hostage to their teenagers' whims, since teenagers often try to solve the problem of feeling inadequate by purchasing items that they do not need or want.

Because teenagers are not financially independent, they usually have to go to their parents for money. Teenagers legally receive money through the following methods:

- Allowances
- After-school jobs
- Summer jobs
- Gifts from friends and family.

Unfortunately, not all teenagers stay within the law. Some teenagers seek greater profits through illegal means. For example, a teenager may decide to sell drugs, enter into prostitution, or engage in some other illegal activity. Teenagers might decide to live on the edge: they may not go beyond the limits of the law, but they may go right up to the limits.

"Because many teenagers see money in highly symbolic terms . . . [they] often try to solve the problem of feeling inadequate by purchasing items that they do not need or want."

One way to avoid these types of problems is to speak with your teenager about financial issues. Keep these points in mind when speaking to a teenager about money:

- Before a financial crash, discuss what not to do with personal finances
- Discuss what to do to prevent a crash
- Set an example for your teenager regarding your own personal finances
- Know that "No" is a legitimate response to your teenager
- Do not give in to their demands

- Provide work for your teenager at home
- Provide counterexamples when your adolescent demands to be allowed to do what his or her friends do
- Make sure that your children understand the worth of money
- Offer choices such as, for example, X compensation for Y grades, or that the adolescent can have A but will lose B
- Find other legal ways for the adolescent to earn necessary money. For example, help your teen to find a job.
- Teach your children to buy only what they can afford. Credit cards can be addictive!
- Teach teenagers to read in between the lines of financial situations and deals
- Do not take a loan just to make your teenager happy
- Do not be ashamed to say to your children that you cannot afford an item
- Do not fear letting a teen fail financially, as bailouts only lead to fiscal irresponsibility.

These principles are given more or less in the order of each "lesson's" complexity, in our estimation. This is probably the order in which we would present these principles to our own children as they mature. For instance, we may facilitate their ability to earn their spending money through home duties at an early age before we would encourage that they work outside the home, and we would then help them find regular part-time employment when they are legally old enough.

When a Financial Crash Happens

Unfortunately, even the best parents must at times face the reality that their children have been financially irresponsible. Once a financial crash has occurred, consider taking some of these actions:

- Review the event so that the teenager understands what happened
- Stand for something, and do not be afraid to be judgmental. Remember, you are the child's parent, and not a friend.
- Use an appropriate punishment. Do not react out of emotions; rather, be in control.
- Insist that your child find a way to compensate for the error.

The last point is, perhaps, the most important of the four because it should reinforce the lesson to be learned from the financial failure the child just experienced.

Tools to Help a Teenager Avoid a Crash

Like everyone else, teenagers need to learn financial planning and how to live within their means. One good way to assimilate good financial habits is to start with a simple budget, like the example in Table 6.1.

Giving teenagers the means to earn some income, and to spend or save according to a budget, will prepare them for financial responsibility as adults.

THE MIDLIFE CRISIS

Psychologists sometimes refer to people who enter into a midlife crisis during their fourth decade of life as "second teenagers" because forty-year-olds have a tendency to return to the abnormalities of adolescents. For instance, men in this age group frequently get divorced and end up paying alimony and/or child support. Other financial problems of forty-year-olds can range from buying big-ticket items that they cannot afford to quitting their jobs and simply running away from life.

Table 6.1. Simple monthly budget for teenagers

ELEMENTS OF A BUDGET	PRACTICAL LINE ITEMS
+Income	**+Income source**
Monthly disposable income	Monthly allowances
Other income sources	After-school jobs or employment
-Expenses	**-Expenses (less than income)**
Regular monthly expenses	For cell phone, dates and recreation, school trips, birthday/holiday gifts
Surprise monthly expenses	Miscellaneous one-time purchases
=Surplus/savings	**=Savings**
Short-term savings	Special desired purchases, big ticket purchases (like a car)
Long-term savings	Educational needs, summer camp, investments/bonds
A child or minor should never run a deficit!	

The Before

Just as in the world of teenagers, midlifers may manifest multiple financial problems that lead to a personal crash. They may use money as a means to avoid the aging process. Family members may feel as though they are held hostage to the midlifers' whims and can become frustrated because, no matter what they do, these people never seem to be happy. Midlifers might then go on to make costly money mistakes just when their ability to recover has been drastically reduced.

Unlike teenagers, midlifers are financially independent, but we do not always see them as acting in the most adult ways. Because they often feel lonely, frustrated, or scared, these people tend to spend money to avoid confronting reality.

The following principles reflect how our attitudes impact our financial situation, and they also comprise a list of things to do before a crash:

1. **Do not compare your life and accomplishments with the lives and accomplishments of other people**. Learn to live within your budget rather than spend money that you do not have. Do not try to "keep up with the Joneses."

2. **Do not seek external validation**. At work, be your own best judge. It does not matter what others say about you. What matters is what you do.

3. **Have a sense of self, and know who you are.** Although you do not have to satisfy everyone, you also do not want to be totally self-centered. Some people will never be pleased. That's because what they are saying does not have much to do with you at all. Do not obsess over pleasing everyone. What others say is nothing more than an outer reflection of their lives and how they feel.

4. **Avoid negative voices.** Never forget that what you allow into your mind will affect you. So be selective, and choose the positive! If you hang out with negative people, you too will become negative. Staying optimistic is not easy when pessimism is the default mode in your world. Not every business venture is a success. Think long term rather than short term.

5. **Avoid looking for a magic bullet.** Economic success depends on hard work rather than pure luck. An economic problem may arise suddenly, but may take years to solve. Be prepared in business.

6. **Do not worry about the past.** In the world of money, it is a waste of time to dwell on past mistakes or "could haves." Learn from your mistake and be future-oriented rather than dwelling on past errors.

7. **Filter your data, because not all data are important.** Your number-one financial resource is time. You can drown in data or use them to your advantage. A smart financial plan entails knowing which data are important and which have nothing to do with your finances.

8. **You are entitled to nothing, so get to work.** Your financial health depends less on the prestige of others (like parents or associates) than on the quality of your work. Complaining is a waste of time, so use your time to produce rather than to demand something from others.

9. **Do not make everything personal, because it's not all about you!** Understand that the market does not depend on you; rather, you have to depend on the financial undulations of the market. Pay attention to financial indicators and learn to read between the lines. Never depend on only one source of information. The best person to analyze your financial situation is you.

10. **Prioritize and determine what is important in your life.** Everyone lives multiple lives. You must decide how much attention you wish to give to family, to your finances, and to yourself. Set priorities and know that every decision has consequences. Your mental state determines the quality of your decisions. Simply being present at a meeting is worthless if you are not concentrating on the task at hand. Remember that you determine the meaning of success in your life.

11. **Do not make your economic problem worse than it seems.** Economies go through ups and downs. Instead of panicking, remember that smart people make money in a down economy.

12. Expect the best, but also be prepared for the worst!
When developing a budget, plan for success but be prepared for failure. Have an alternate and some money put away for that proverbial "rainy day."

These twelve principles for midlifers can also apply to other people. They are common sense but you need to apply them *before* a financial crisis happens.

Tools to Help a Midlifer Avoid a Crash

Although most adults will have worked with some sort of budget by their midlives, they may want to reassess their skills and habits. And, for those who have been lax, it is not too late to start budgeting effectively.

Exercise 6.1. Create or update a monthly budget

Table 6.1 and Table 6.2 provide models of personal budgets for teenagers, single midlifers, and those with more complex family considerations. The line items are suggested categories that you may name differently or exclude entirely. You may also have categories of income, expenses, or savings that we have not listed here. But the tables should cover most of the categories that are needed in a personal budget.

Use the blank worksheet shown in Appendix A.12 on page 157 if you do not already have your own budgeting template, or if you want to create an entirely new one. The downloadable version of this worksheet is in Microsoft Excel format and performs automatic calculations for you (see page 157).

If you have an existing budget, review and compare it with either Table 6.1 or Table 6.2 to determine where your financial strengths and weaknesses are.

Make an effort to improve your spending and saving habits. This will go a long way toward helping you to avoid a financial crash.

Table 6.2. Monthly budgets for midlifers

SINGLE PERSON	COUPLE OR FAMILY
+Income	**+Income**
Salary	Salary
Second job	Second job
Bank account interest earnings	Bank account interest earnings
Savings disbursements	Savings disbursements
	Gains from stocks and bonds
	Other salaries or earnings
	Inheritances
− Expenses	**− Expenses**
Rent or mortgage	Rent or mortgage
Transportation costs	Transportation costs
Insurance	Insurance
Medical and dental	Medical and dental
Clothing	Clothing
Food	Food
Recreation	Recreation
Debts and credit card payments	Debts and credit card payments
Communications (phones, etc.)	Communications (phones, etc.)
Taxes	Taxes
Professional growth or reeducation	Professional growth or reeducation
	Children's educational needs
= Savings	**= Savings**
Short-term savings	Short-term savings
Retirement plans and savings	Retirement plans and savings
Vacations	Vacations, summer camps
Investments/bonds	Investments/bonds

When a Financial Crash Happens

The fourth decade of life can be a time when we not only live on the edge, but also fall off the edge. Undoubtedly, people in their forties often provoke their own crises.

Unfortunately, midlifers are not children, and their parents cannot solve their problems. People in their forties are legally responsible for their debts and economic mistakes. Therefore, the following principles are essential when a midlifer is forced to face fiscal reality:

- Face the fact that you are in a difficult financial bind
- Evaluate the situation and see whether you can solve it by yourself
- Do not be arrogant. If you need help, seek it.
- Do not be afraid of what others may say
- See whether you can lower expenses and/or increase earnings.

When a financial crisis happens, ask yourself the following questions and apply your responses to a new budget in order to get back on the road to discovery:

- Where are you spending too much?
- Where can you cut back?
- Does your income equal your expenses? If not, how are you making up for the shortfall?
- Are you spending money simply to cover up a psychological problem?
- Are you using credit cards to pay for things that you cannot afford?

Consider finding an organization that can help you get back on track. Speak with your accountant and lawyer about someone who might be able to put your financial house in order. Many national agencies also offer financial advice (at a cost). Some of these are the National Association of Personal Financial Advisors (NAPFA), Ameriprise Financial, and Wiseradviser. The authors of this book do not intend to recommend any particular adviser. Remember to be truthful with whoever your adviser is. An adviser can help only if he or she knows all the facts of your financial situation.

If the situation cannot be solved, consider the possibility of bankruptcy. If bankruptcy occurs, see it as a learning opportunity and start again.

THE RETIREE

We turn now to those who are entering their golden years and for whom the key to developing a successful retirement is successful planning. Do not wait until you are in your sixties to start saving. Retirement is not a simple process. It takes planning and hard work.

The Before

Take note of the results of a survey that examines Americans' retirement preparation practices. According to Selena Maranjian (2007) of *The Motley Fool*, the findings of the survey are as follows:

- Thirty-six percent of women and twenty-nine percent of men indicated that "they worry about retirement 'all the time'"
- Thirty-six percent of women and forty-eight percent of men said that "they are well prepared for retirement"
- Forty-nine percent of women revealed that "they save less than five percent of their total income last year" and that "half as many women as men save more than ten percent of their annual income"
- Twenty-three percent of women and seventeen percent of men "who have a retirement plan available to them at work do not participate at all in that plan"
- Fifty-five percent of men and forty-one percent of women "have a brokerage account"

- Women reported often feeling "'intimidated' and 'over-whelmed' by the thought of investing"
- "Sixty percent of women and forty-five percent of men have no financial game plan at all."

These statistics make it clear that most people do not prepare enough—or, in many cases, at all—for retirement. When we couple these figures with the fact that most women will outlive their husbands, the potential for economic disaster becomes all the greater. The time to start is any time before retirement, but the earlier, the better. It is never too soon. So, if you are not already retired, now is the time to start a plan or to revisit your existing plan.

A financial retirement plan begins with serious introspection about your life goals and what you expect you will want to do upon retirement. Will your time be consumed with younger generations in your family? Or perhaps with pursuing spiritual or lifelong hobbies and interests?

Those are the higher-level considerations about how you plan to use your time in retirement. To achieve your goals, you will need enough money to support the activities that you envision.

You will also need to think about the issues and problems that are common for people in their golden years. These issues can, and frequently do, disrupt the best-laid retirement plans.

The following exercise is meant to focus your mind on many of the issues that you may well need to contend with during your retirement. These issues can affect you, a spouse, or another loved one.

Exercise 6.2. Create a post-retirement resources plan
There are issues to think about and prepare before a retirement-age crisis occurs. First, let's take a minute to ponder some very important preretirement issues.

- How much money do you have saved?
- What is the health diagnosis for your family? (Our parents' health and longevity provide good clues to our future problems.)
- Is there a particular illness in your family? Do you have a history of cancer or other diseases?
- What will be your income sources? In retirement, it is more about expenses than income.
- In what region or city do you want to live? What is the cost of living in that area?
- Do you have younger people to help you?
- Can you depend on your children, or do they depend on you?
- Where do you get financial advice?
- Have you planned for a debilitating mental illness, such as dementia?
- Where will you live when you can no longer care for yourself?

After you finish this mental exercise, you will be ready to compose a plan for your post-retirement needs and resources, as illustrated in Figure 6.1. Use the blank worksheet shown in Appendix A.13 on page 160 to complete your plan. The downloadable version of this worksheet is in Microsoft Excel format and performs automatic calculations for you (see page 158).

The After

Unfortunately, things do not always work out the way that we had hoped they would. Too often, retirement turns out to be less than we expected.

Although not impossible, economic recovery is more diffi-cult when a crisis occurs in the final decades of life. When prob-lems occur, retired people report feelings of aloneness, of being abandoned or mistreated, and a sense that they have been "warehoused." Here are some ideas about what to do should you find yourself in that situation:

Figure 6.1. Post-retirement resources worksheet

Potential Issues	Mitigating Strategy	Desired Outcome
Spouse's family has history of dementia and/or cancer at age 75 on	Purchase /maintain a long-term care insurance policy	Ins. policy with benefits equivalent to $65K income
My existing AF prevents me from getting long-term care insurance	Assure that retirement age resources are high enough to cover long-term care if necessary	$75K/year retirement income for me
Cannot depend on grown children, who have limited income and large families	Provide available disposable income before and upon retirement for grandkids' ed.	Pass our retirement savings to children upon death

Retirement Resources Needed	Manner of Acquisition	Planned For Savings
Spouse's 401K plan	Working years contributions	$750,000
My 401K plan (or similar)	Working years contributions	$600,000
Stocks and bonds	Working years purchases	$250,000
Subtotal of Planned Retirement Resources Needed		$1,600,000

Minus

Personal Savings/Investments	Manner of Acquisition	Current Savings
Spouse's 401K savings	Contributions from wages	$552,000
My 401K Savings	Contributions from wages	$375,000
Stocks and bonds	Disposable income purchases	$55,000
Subtotal of Current Retirement Resources		$982,000

Equals

CURRENT SHORTFALL	$618,000
TIME LEFT TO RETIRE/ACCRUE THROUGH FOLLOWING:	11 years (132 mo.)
Deductions/savings from earnings to 401K plans	$550/mo.
Employer contributions to 401K plans	$550/mo.
Investments from disposable income	$1,000/mo.

Employer/Govt. Annuities	Manner of Acquisition	Expected Value
Spouse's Social Security $	Qualified through work history	$20,000/year
My Social Security $	Qualified through work history	$20,000/year
My Annuity	Employer's retirement plan	$50,000/year
Subtotal of Sponsored Plans		$90,000/year

Plus

Yearly retirement income distribution of 5% from Retirement Resources	$80,000
TOTAL PLANNED RETIREMENT INCOME (PRESENT VALUE)	$170,000

- Do not try to solve these problems by yourself. Seek expert help and get two or three separate opinions. Be cautious, because there are many people who will take advantage of the elderly.
- Do everything that you can to maintain social contacts
- Volunteer or become involved in a religious organization
- If you trust your children, ask one of them to accompany you when you speak with a financial expert
- Contact social services if you are at an assisted living home and feel that you are being abused
- Do not be afraid to get the advice of a pastor, priest, rabbi, or other spiritual leader. These people can usually put you in contact with the proper financial professional.
- Speak to someone at your local Social Security office
- Do not be afraid to ask for medical assistance
- Ask a trusted relative or friend to help you develop a budget
- Make sure that your last will and testament is in order
- Concentrate on beautiful memories rather than allowing yourself to become bitter.

Should your problem be something other than—or in addition to—loneliness or abuse, then as a first step, it may be helpful to *(a)* articulate the issues as best as you can, *(b)* and then identify possible, actionable solutions that *(c)* a trusted friend, family member, or a professional, can help you carry out. Here are some additional pointers that may be useful for people of retirement age in particular to keep in mind:

Save! Save! Save! Put away as much money as you can at the earliest age possible. Do not depend on your retirement fund exclusively, especially now that so many governments are going broke. That retirement fund may not be there when you need it.

Buying in bulk is not always wise. Unless you have a very large family or eat large amounts of a specific type of food, most bulk buying is a waste of money. You may well lose more in spoilage than you gained in savings.

Distribute your money in as many places as possible. Banks today are far from safe. Use them, but also be cautious of them.

Never buy what you cannot afford, and avoid credit cards like the plague. There is no worse interest rate than that of a credit card. If you cannot afford to pay for something at that moment, then do not buy it.

Take vitamins and see a doctor on a regular basis. There is nothing more expensive than getting sick. Stay healthy by exercising and keeping your stress levels as low as you can.

RECOVERING FROM A FINANCIAL CRISIS

Sometimes, a financial crash is not the result of a personal shortcoming, such as a crash that is caused by an unexpected life-threatening illness in the family. However, in some situations, we have to assume responsibility. For example, did we take out a mortgage that we could not afford to pay? Did we purchase items that were beyond our budget or that caused us to incur so much debt that bankruptcy became the only solution?

Financial crashes are most likely the result of poor spending habits or the lack of a personal financial plan. Once you have analyzed your spending habits, you may have one more step to take toward achieving responsible personal finances: You need a personal budget plan and a way to track your money against it, if you are not already doing so (or, perhaps, you need a new financial plan). This will help you to live within your means, and it will go a long way toward preventing another financial crisis.

Simple Online Financial-Planning Tools

Fortunately, there are many easy ways to do this today with nothing more than a smartphone, although a personal computer or tablet is preferable, at least to set up an online account. You will only need the temporary use of a computer with Internet access to go online, sign up for a service, and set up your account. Once that is done, you can track and maintain your finances with just a smartphone.

The easiest way to set up a budget and track money against it is to use one of many free personal finance apps (that is, "applications" or services) online. Some offer only free accounts or a free basic service with options to upgrade to more features; some offer only fee-based accounts. We have tried many such services, and we continue to test new ones regularly.

The following are the top three online personal finance apps available for free or for a minimal cost, according to Jim Wang (2017) of *Wallet Hacks*, a well-regarded reviewer of Internet-based apps:

Mint.com can be set up to read information from one or more accounts from nearly any US bank or financial institution. It then automatically presents to the user a variety of reports, such as a personal net worth, balances of individual accounts, a budget plan, and cash flow. Once set up, it requires minimal effort from the user. Mint.com includes excellent sections for budgeting, setting long-term goals, and bill payments, and all of these sections of the user's account are integrated.

Mint.com is a colorful app, and its free price means that you will need to endure relevant financial-oriented advertisements for tax preparation or new banking services, for example. But the ads are not excessive, and you may well want to pursue some of the offerings.

Personal Capital (personalcapital.com) is very similar to mint. com but presents information in a more traditional, cleaner interface. It is also free, so it also contains advertisements but, as with the advertisements in mint.com, they are not highly intrusive.

You Need A Budget or YNAB (youneedabudget.com) is another excellent online app that is simple to set up and use. Although the first two apps on this list also have strong budgeting modules, this one is budget-centric; that is, its setup starts with the creation of a budget, and then the app's services remain focused on making every dollar that passes in or out count by comparing each transaction against the budget. This app, however, is not free. It costs just over $4.00 per month (at the time of publication), but you can try it for free during the first month. The yearly cost for this service is approximately $50.00.

For that very reasonable fee, you get an advertisement-free service, a very clean user interface, and something that the free services do not provide—namely, the ability to add and maintain accounts manually, so that you can choose to create an account manually and track monies through it, and run all other accounts through the automatic data feeds from banks. Neither mint.com nor Personal Capital can do that.

You could need to set up an account manually if your bank does not yet participate in sending online data feeds to a third-party (in this case, the service app of your choice, such as YNAB).

The manual account setup is espeially useful becasue it can be used in many ways, such as to track medical insurance copayments due and made, and to track personal loans and payments that you make or receive.

A word of caution about using mint.com, Personal Capital, YNAB, and other similar services is necessary, though. Be sure to back up your account's data regularly (at least quarterly), for two reasons: first, your data that is stored with any online service (or on your computer) can become corrupted; and, second, these online apps do not store your account data perpetually. Transaction histories generally go back no more than three years. So, you will need to employ a data retention strategy by exporting your data regularly to something like an electronic spreadsheet that you keep. If you need to, the information can then be printed on paper reports or used in electronic spreadsheet format.

As a matter of full disclosure, these recommendations are made entirely from our own experiences with various financial systems. We have no connection with any of these services other than having been or being customers ourselves, and we derive no compensation from them.

You are encouraged to visit *Wallet Hack* yourself to read the entire review that includes the top ten apps. But remember that the fast-paced Internet environment may well change the apps landscape by the time that you read this publication. Your own online search may identify newer, better financial apps then.

We would be remiss not to mention that we are also familiar with bank-provided personal financial apps. Our assessment of those is that they vary in usefulness. Your bank's money-management offering may be just as capable—or more so—as the three apps that are mentioned in this section, and they may have the added advantage of allowing you to track and budget electronically, right from your principal checking account.

To start your new personal finances program, take an hour or two to visit these sites, sign up for one or more services, and proceed through a guided setup that walks you through their step-by-step process. It is nearly painless, and all you will need is your banking login information. You may want to sign up for all three to see which one is most to your liking.

Old-Fashioned Financial-Planning Tools

If online or computer-based programs and services are not what you feel comfortable with, there are always offline or paper-based money management systems.

Paper-based tools would include an old-fashioned check register to track checking account transactions, including debit card purchases; paper statements for savings or investment accounts; and a paper-based budget sheet, like the one that is illustrated in Table 6.2 on page 89 and provided as a blank form in Appendix A.12 on page 157.

Creating a budget is easier and more accurate when you use a programmed, electronic budget calculator, which is available for you to download (in Excel format) at quest-publishing.com/resources/personal-reconstruction.

Manually tracking money and setting spending and savings goals can be cumbersome and may lead to errors. But it is how people have managed their money until recently, and it may be how you want to manage your finances now.

■ ■ ■

In summary, how we handle our money tells us a great deal about who we are. Are we responsible with our own resources and other people's money? Do we seek loans that we know we cannot repay? Do we gamble with our own financial health or with the health of other people?

Unlike issues of spirituality, finances are much more precise. Our actions regarding our finances are an insight into the quality of our character. As such, our finances are intertwined with our sense of spirituality: They reflect our psychological state and, if mishandled, they can turn into issues of law.

C H A P T E R

7

THE LAW IN OUR LIVES

At his best, man is the noblest of all animals;
separated from law and justice he is the worst.

— Aristotle

A S LONG AS human beings have existed, there have been laws in place in one form or another. Well before any writing or languages were developed, those who were stronger, greater in numbers, or in control of resources, were able to impose their will on others.

As time passed and human beings began living in larger groups, there came a need to establish a greater level of order so that society could live with a lessened level of risk, violence, and problems. That ushered in legal frameworks that enabled people to achieve progress and live in a less stressful environment.

Without laws, there would be limited, if any, protections against wrongdoers of all types. You would be hesitant to go to work. After all, who would guard your household and belonging while you were out working? Would you really want to take a bus to work if that bus did not have to be maintained according to a basic safety code? How would a bank be able to lend you money to buy a house if rules were not in place to make that bank conform to requirements such as paying interest on your accounts and insuring the safety of your deposits? How would you get to the bank on the roads if there were no traffic rules? And on and on it goes.

A society's laws (and enforcement mechanisms) make it possible for its members to depend on each other to carry out individual responsibilities and go about their complex daily rituals, and to settle disagreements or dishonored commitments peacefully.

THE LAW IN GENERAL

Laws can be confusing; they can be burdensome or even senseless; and they can be contradictory to common sense, maddening, or even downright ridiculous sometimes. But laws are not unnecessary, for without them, as Thomas Hobbes (2012) wrote in 1651, life would be "nasty, brutish, and short." The legal system may change, but one thing that has been and will remain a constant is the fact that the law is a part of our lives.

It is important that we as members of a society have at least a basic working knowledge about how laws originate and are categorized into two main bodies: civil and criminal.

The Origins of Laws

In the United States and many other countries, laws are rules that are created by a government that is elected by the citizens of the community. The legal system does not care about how you feel, what you want, or what happened in your past that makes you who you are today. What the law does care about is whether you choose to do what it is legally correct to do when you are faced with a *legal crossroad*—a moment at which you make a decision that has long-term legal implications. Nothing more; nothing less.

We have all faced legal crossroads, and we have all made both good and bad choices and paid a price; but some bad choices stand out and cause us particular grief. It is important to understand that we must keep a reasonable level of expectation for ourselves and for others when it comes to legal decision making.

There are literally thousands of laws on the books, and it is impossible even for a licensed attorney to memorize them all and follow them strictly. By simply driving a car at any given time, one is likely to be in violation of a traffic law in some form or another by signaling too late, speeding, parking too far from a curb, etc. It is impossible never to break a law, and it would be unreasonable for a person to expect that of him- or herself or others.

It has been said that America is the land of 50,000 laws to help us follow the ten commandments. In other words, it is important to have an understanding of the big picture when it comes to legal decisions, and to evaluate any potential decision-making event through a lens of knowing right from wrong.

"It is impossible never to break a law, and it would be unreasonable for a person to expect that of him- or herself or others . . . [But] it is important to have an understanding of the big picture [and know] right from wrong."

Following the law is not as easy as one would think. In essence, following the law means following the customs that ordinary people would define as doing "right" versus doing "wrong."

Civil Law Versus Criminal Law

Criminal law is similar to civil law in many ways but different in others. Although both criminal matters and civil matters are heard in courts, and both are ultimately governed by our Constitution, in a criminal case the accused faces the possibility of the restriction or loss of their liberty. Criminal cases can be minor—such as for traffic tickets or fines for littering—or can involve years in prison, probation, or even a death penalty.

Running afoul of the law won't open any doors for you, but it sure can close them, sometimes forever. So, it is important for us to look at our relationship with the law as it relates to the financial, spiritual, and psychological parts of ourselves.

EXAMPLES OF CRIME CONSEQUENCES

A criminal conviction can cost a lot in terms of freedom, money, rights, and lost opportunities in life. The consequences are many, like:

- Going to jail or prison for a long time.
- Pay heavy financial penalties to the court or restitution to a victim.
- Lose the right to vote.
- Lose the right to own a firearm.
- Be prevented from military service.
- Be prevented from taking a job at institutions that handle controlled substances or money.
- If convicted of child abuse or a sex offense, lose the right to live within a certain distance of a school or playground.

As society evolves and changes, so does the criminal legal system. In the 1850s, horse theft was a real problem and was punished severely because horses were many people's main mode of transportation. Today, it is still a crime to steal a horse, but the frequency of horse theft and the severity of the punishment for it are much lower. Conversely, there were no laws against online harassment in the 1850s because the Internet did not exist. It was not even a concept in the minds of lawmakers then.

Civil law covers anything to do with going to court for any purpose other than to find someone guilty or not guilty of a crime.

To review the consequences of a civil law case, let's turn back to our earlier example about a restaurant that keeps a dirty kitchen or serves unsafe food. Sooner or later, the restaurant owner will lose his or her license to operate a restaurant altogether if he or she becomes known to the city health department as a frequent violator. Someone who only knows the restaurant business and is not well suited for other types of work will be out of luck.

Civil cases can be very complex or very simple. They can be about a minor sum of money in small claims court, or a major lawsuit that involves hundreds of thousands of documents with billions of dollars at stake in a battle at the US Supreme Court.

Civil laws exist as a way of resolving disputes in business dealings, family matters, and as a means to regulate the behavior of the public. For instance, if a restaurant regularly keeps a dirty kitchen and serves food that sickens people, then they can face fines and even have their license to operate revoked. Because the owner is operating in a system in which these consequences can happen, the owner will likely take steps to prevent such a problem. He or she is likely to keep the kitchen clean and food fresh to avoid losing the business or risk the restaurant's good reputation for following the rules that the law demands must be followed.

The goal of civil laws is to deter people from harmful or

problematic behavior by having a means in place to discipline and fine them for not conforming to laws in place for the general welfare of the public.

EXAMPLES OF CIVIL CASES

- Suing a driver for hitting your car with his car.

- Fighting a custody battle or filing for a divorce.

- Suing an employer for wrongfully firing you..

- Asking a court to order your neighbor to stop working on his fence until the property line is established..

- Dealing with a bankruptcy.

The most important common feature between civil and criminal law is that both can result in consequences, however light or severe, that last well into a person's future, or perhaps even the rest of a person's life.

THE LAW AND IN-VISIONING

If you have jumped straight to this chapter before reading the chapters about finance, spirituality, and psychology, then you should go back and read them first, because the material here is knitted into those aspects of your life.

Remember that the purpose of in-visioning is to look at yourself and your decision-making skills in a broader context. How do finance, spirituality, and psychology tie into a person's legal decision making? Let's explore that.

Working Through Legal Problems

The best way to deal with legal problems is to avoid having them in the first place. Sometimes, your legal problem happens because you are a victim of someone else's bad decision making or lack of spiritual, financial, or psychological well-being. However, you may be in court as the result of your own doing, or simply to settle a dispute. In any case, even if you already have had legal problems, it is best to conform your behavior so as to avoid having new ones.

Although it may not be apparent at first, playing by the rules is usually much easier than not doing so. The long-term costs usually far outweigh the immediate benefits of breaking a law or regulation.

Legal problems are not always avoidable. Like it or not, you will sometimes need to deal with the judicial system. One of the most important issues that you will face is the question of legal representation. Although you always have the right to represent yourself in a legal matter, generally speaking it is not a good idea to do so. There is a saying that "any lawyer who represents himself has a fool for a client." It may seem like a good idea to represent yourself in order to save money on legal fees, but there is a tremendous amount of value in having a knowledgeable professional who is not emotionally connected to the outcome of the case to handle the matter for you.

Regardless of whether you are suing, being sued, or defending yourself in a criminal case, the outcome of the case is likely going to significantly impact your future and the rest of your life. Courtrooms are places where major life events happen, and it is important when you are in court that you have someone there who has your best interests at heart, who is skilled and capable of effectuating those best interests when it is most important to do so.

When a Lawyer Is Necessary

One factor that you should consider when choosing a lawyer is price. Many practicing lawyers charge surprisingly small fees. For something like a traffic ticket, one can hardly justify charging a lot of money. But for more serious matters, particularly of the criminal variety, it is important that a person be represented by a counsel who is serious and dedicated to achieving results.

There are twenty-four hours in a day, and when a lawyer charges small fees for serious cases, it is usually because that lawyer makes his or her money on the volume of cases rather than by charging higher fees for fewer cases. So, when it comes time to taking hours out of that twenty-four-hour day, how much time is that lawyer really spending on your case? Is the lawyer dedicating fewer hours to a greater number of clients? How much time and effort can he or she allocate to you?

Lawyers' services are like anything else: you generally get what you pay for. Make it a point to interview a number of different lawyers and to ask questions directly of those whom you are considering hiring. Find the lawyer whom you think is best suited to tell your story and gives you a feeling of trust and confidence.

When talking to prospective lawyers, be sure to tell them what your goals are, and be sure to listen to their responses when they tell you how realistic or possible achieving those goals is. A realistic view of what you are dealing with goes a long way toward making sure that you have good attorney-client relations, something that is not lost on a jury if and when your case is judged at trial.

Support Networks

Depending on the type of case, it is important to maintain good relations with friends and family, not just for spiritual and psychological purposes, but also because they can be invaluable witnesses on your behalf during a court case. Those who love and care about you want to help. It is important to listen to them and appreciate them. Dealing with a case can be stressful, so do your best not to alienate the people in your life by taking out your stress and anxiety on them.

CROSSROADS AND CONSEQUENCES

When people break laws, they also give up opportunities. Perceiving the violation of laws that way lets us analyze our actions from the perspective of how much more we give up in the long run by breaking laws than we gain in the short term.

When we face legal crossroads, we also face a decision about whether to do something, despite or because of the legal consequences that we face. Each of us has found ourselves at such a crossroad, and we have all made good and bad choices at some of those crossroads. With each choice comes a consequence.

How Law Affects Your Daily Life

Below is a list of the types of laws that often come into play in daily living for most of us. Let's look at them one at a time and apply how the spiritual, financial, and emotional pillars of life interact with the legal pillar.

Family and matrimonial law. When we choose to live with or marry someone, do we do so out of obligation or love or for money? Or do we do so because of all four aspects of our lives—that is, for a balance of law, psychology, finance, and spirituality? Are we giving the needs of the other person the same importance as our own? What about the needs of children and family? How does parenting balance out with being a good partner?

Employment law. Are we avoiding things like sexual harassment, creating a hostile work environment, or ignoring discrimination? Are we in compliance with the laws and regulations on the books for disabled people, parents of newborn children, and veterans? Is the work environment safe and up to code?

Criminal law. This can entail everything from obeying traffic laws to keeping out of jail or prison. Criminal laws are often the most "common sense" ones to follow.

The questions posed here should illustrate how psychology, spirituality, and finances mix into the legal realm. In fact, laws are just the written rules for governing our behavior in the three other areas of our lives.

Improving Your Decision Making

This chapter will not solve the already-existing problems in your life that have come as a result of not choosing the right path when you were at a legal crossroads in your past. What this chapter seeks to do is to recondition your thinking so that when you inevitably arrive at another legal crossroads in the future, you will recall the exercises in this chapter, remember the thoughts and feelings that you associate with these exercises, and then take the right path. This chapter's goal is to apply to the legal-crossroad decisions that you face that famous axiom from Benjamin Franklin: "An ounce of prevention is worth a pound of cure."

You may be the type of person who generally makes good choices in life. Or you may be a person who once made poor choices, then learned from them, and now avoids making the types of bad choices that caused you so many problems in the past.

If you have already made some particularly bad choices when you stood at a legal crossroad, then this chapter will help you gain perspective and grow as a person who has learned from the past. It will help prevent you from repeating the cycle of bad choices.

Remember that this book does not dispense legal advice, does not create an attorney-client relationship, and is not a one-size-fits-all answer to any and every legal issue that our readers face. This chapter is only a guide for you to use as you make decisions when you face legal crossroads.

People often seek counseling or therapy because they are trying to deal with issues that continually cause them problems in their lives. These issues often recur and can be caused by anything from a difficult childhood to a lost loved one, or addiction, and so on.

This book is not a psychoanalysis tool. What it is meant to do is to cause us, as individuals, to look within ourselves and analyze how we have made choices in the past, and to look at the resulting good and bad legal consequences, and their effects on our lives. If this is your case, now is the time to take stock of your situation.

Exercise 7.1. Assess your legal-crossroads situation

Use the blank worksheet shown in Appendix A.14 on page 159 to assess your own legal crossroads. See Figure 7.1 for an illustration of how you may complete this exercise.

On the left side of your worksheet, list up to ten of the most consequential legal crossroads that you have faced. Then, while answering the following questions, list in the right column the long-term consequence (cost or benefit) that you derived from the choice made. These questions that you should consider in building these lists are:

- What possible actions would you take in response to these hurts?
- What were the advantages of the way that you reacted?
- What were the disadvantages of the way that you reacted?
- Within these situations, over which parts did you have control? When the situation has come to its termination, what would you like to feel?

Your entries in both columns should give you some clues about how your past behavior has led to (or helped you avoid) unwanted consequences. Can you tell what emotions have been behind your decisions? If you recognize the emotional trigger behind your bad decisions, can you learn to control yourself and your behavior the next time you come to a legal crossroad?

Figure 7.1. Legal crossroads assessment worksheet

Use this form to create a list of legal crossroads you have faced	
Bad choices made (or wanted to do but did not) while at a legal crossroad	Negative consequences (lost opportunities and other costs) that resulted (or would have) from bad choices
Have been stopped several times for speeding and reckless driving.	Have had to pay about $500 per year in traffic fines, plus $250 for traffic school to not lose license, and auto insurance became $450 higher per year than a safe driver's.
Refused to pay court-ordered alimony and child support because my ex doesn't deserve it.	I was sued by ex and the court made me pay $15,000 in back payments plus all court costs of $12,000 to stay out of jail for contempt of court.
Considered filing a less-than-honest tax return because the government is taxing way too much of my pay.	If caught, I could have been prosecuted for fraud and tax evasion, and penalized up to $5,000 and jailed for as long as 7 years.
Considered not paying a $4,000 bill because I knew that the amount I was withholding was not enough for the other party to consider suing me.	I would have been reported to credit bureaus, my credit score would have dropped a lot, future credit or loans would have bigger interest rates or would be denied; plus I felt I was cheating the other party.
Really wanted to hit a spouse, lover, or family member for making me really mad about something.	Could have been arrested/prosecuted for assault and battery or domestic abuse; could be jailed; potentially losing custody of my children; and probable damaged relationship with person.
Incarcerated for seven years for something I was accused of.	Am missing out on many years of my children's lives, and times we should be sharing.

What Awareness Is

A substantial part of good decision making is awareness, but being aware does not mean seeing things as they are on an immediate, superficial level. Awareness means looking at everything from a three-dimensional standpoint and assessing the potential risks and rewards.

In contemplating marriage, as one example of an awareness

situation, you need to know not just what your obligations are, but also what you expect your prospective spouse's obligations toward you to be. Does your partner come into the marriage with children? If so, how do you get along with them? Do you and that person have similar financial habits and goals? If not, will this lead to a bad marriage with a potential for violence or bitter custody battles? Are you or that person in debt? Does he or she owe child support? Has he or she had any criminal history, domestic-violence history, or a history with social services? How is this person's credit history? (You may be sharing a mortgage, so this is good to know.) Are there aging parents or relatives to care for, or that social services may place with you? Knowing this and accounting for it early is an essential part of awareness.

Awareness helps you identify issues that you may want to prepare for early on, and awareness is not always easy to develop. Thinking three-dimensionally requires us to see the good, the bad, and the ugly; and many people, particularly people in a new relationship, do not want to do that. It is important to think and to plan on what will come the day after the wedding, or move-in, or birth of a new baby.

Exercise 7.2. Assess your legal stressors

You may want to exercise your awareness now by using the blank worksheet shown in Appendix A.15 on page 160. Figure 7.2 shows you how you can score your worksheet—that is, it helps you to become aware of the actual or potential legal issues in your life. In this example, the score is 22, which suggests that this couple will probably face a normal, manageable level of stress and problems that they should be able to navigate and resolve. However, be aware that our suggested scoring method and scale may or may not be right for you or your circumstances. We believe it to be right for most people, but you should adjust it if you feel that it does not represent your needs.

Figure 7.2. Legal stressors assessment worksheet

ISSUE	YOU	YOUR PARTNER
Child custody/child support	0	4
Opening a new business, starting a new job, going back to school, or a new career path	0	1
Major physical or psychological medical challenge	3	1
Major credit or financial change/challenge	1	3
Criminal case or incarceration	4	0
Having to care for or be a guardian for relatives outside the nuclear family	0	3
Serious debt or bankruptcy	0	0
Children from previous relationship is/are facing challenges	0	2
Nothing else to add		
INDIVIDUAL SCORES	8	14
COMBINED SCORE		22

Scale:	0 = None / 1 =Maybe / 2 = Possible / 3 = Probable / 4 = Certain
Scoring:	0 to 13 points = no forecasted stressors for the relationship
	14 to 26 points = expect some points of contention to work through
	27 to 39 points = expect a need to overcome manageable issues
	40 to 52 points = expect a very stressed relationship unlikely to survive
	53 plus points = expect a highly challenged relationship very unlikely to survive

Raising Awareness

It goes without saying that a significant aspect of being aware is knowing what to look for in the first place. It is difficult to spot a red flag, for instance, if we do not know much about the particular area of law in which that red flag may become a real problem.

The law is a broad and, at times, complex subject, and many of us do not know nearly as much about it as we think we do. Considering that the law and how we relate to it in the decision-making process can have such a major effect on our lives, it is worth assessing how much we think we know about the law versus how much we really know about it. Consider the areas of law that are listed in the "Legal" column of Table 7.1 that can impact our day-to-day lives. How much do you really know about each of those areas of law?

It may be that some of these legal areas do not apply to your daily life at all and perhaps never will. For example, a person who plans on remaining unmarried and having no children probably will never need to know much about issues in the context of family law such as divorce or custody of children. Still, life can throw us curve balls and bring surprises and real change. It is worth being clear with yourself about how much you know about these diverse areas of law.

Now let's examine how being self-centered (egocentric) diminishes our legal awareness (and other aspects of life) and can put our lives out of balance. This character trait is one of the chief problems in developing legal awareness, and is likely to lead us into problematic situations. In other words, egocentric people believe that they are the center of the world, and that they know best about every situation, including legal ones.

Earlier in this chapter, we talked about the origin of law as a means of enabling us to live together as a community. Laws are the common set of rules that keep our behaviors as a society in order. Laws are about more than just us as individuals.

If we are egocentric, then we do not understand that we are not alone, that we need laws to guide us. In order to lead balanced lives, we need a healthy balance of legal awareness along with emotional, financial, and spiritual awareness. The ways in which legal matters affect the other areas of your life are illustrated in Table 7.1.

Table 7.1. How legal matters affect your life

LEGAL	FINANCIAL	SPIRITUAL	PSYCHOLOGICAL
Family/ Domestic law	• Prevents loss or division of assets • Retains retirement account integrity • Manages/prevents debt problems	• Intact families raise more spiritual children • Better family life = greater appreciation for what we have	• Intact families are happier • Fewer family problems lead to better health
Employment law	• Promotes positive work environments • Works for promotions and raises • Prevents or manages debt issues	• Work satisfaction increases spiritual fulfillment • More income means more money for charities & tithes	• Less work anxiety = better family life • Less work stress = better health and longer life span
Criminal law	• Criminal problems = legal fees, court costs • Criminal problems = lost jobs or wages • Criminal problems = hiring difficulties	• Criminal problems lead to self-doubt and hopelessness	• Criminal problems = stress on families • Criminal problems = physical health problems and shorten life spans
Insurance law	• Know your coverage limits before a catastrophe occurs • Prevents being over insured or under insured (both costly)	• Peace of mind in knowing you have done right to protect loved ones, the public and assets	• Having insurance allows one to take safe, calculated risks • Insurance coverage minimizes anxiety and stress
Credit/ Consumer rights law	• Knowing your rights can prevent losing money in lawsuits • Knowing your rights can prevent loss to predatory collectors	• Satisfaction in paying what is honestly owed to others • Protecting friends, family from unscrupulous collectors	• Knowing the legal limits a creditor has lowers anxiety • Knowing your rights to relief from collectors lowers anxiety
Estate planning (wills, trusts, guardianship and probate)	• Prevents needless loss of money to taxes • Prevents irresponsible use of money when protecting the future of loved ones	• Allows for more charitable giving	• Knowing that your post-death arrangements for family and assets are and will be well managed lowers anxiety

The purpose of Table 7.1 is to show you the interrelationships between legal matters and its financial, spiritual, and psychological components. A legal choice that we make can—and often does—bleed over into other areas of life.

For instance, if you were to smuggle a large quantity of drugs for a significant fee and are not caught, how would that money affect you spiritually or psychologically? Might you start thinking that something like this is OK and, perhaps, start doing more of it? Would the thought occur to you that each new "job" then increases your chances of being arrested in the future? You would become psychologically out of balance because, in your mind, you would ask yourself why you need to work hard for an honest dollar when quick and easy money is available by carrying drugs. You would become less honest as a person, less ethical, and that would affect you spiritually. You would lose even by winning.

However, if you were caught and arrested, how would that affect you in other areas of life? In that case, you wouldn't keep the money. Instead, you would end up spending a lot of money on your legal defense when a serious case is filed against you. You may face the loss of your children if your significant other divorces you while you are in jail; or you may lose your home if you are unable to pay the mortgage because you are in jail or moneyless because of legal bills and court costs. Even when you get out, it's hard to get a loan or other credit because of your past, and starting a business is not easy because the license that you need from a government entity may be held up or denied because of your background.

Changing the way that you think is what this chapter aims to do. Awareness, to be truly *awareness*, must be three-dimensional. It is critically important to think about the whole-life-impact of every decision that you make when standing at a legal crossroad.

LAW AND MONEY

Perhaps the greatest motivator of poor legal decisions is a desire for more money. Sometimes, that may come out of a sense of desperation or despair over a lack of money for life's needs;

other times, it may come as a result of greed or a desire to feel important. In any case, when it comes to factoring money into the legal-decision-making process, it is very important to take the approach of awareness and of living a balanced life.

Having a desire to earn more money is perfectly fine, even admirable, as money can mean improving oneself and being in a position to help others. The desire for more money is not the problem; it's the decisions that one makes in terms of taking actions to further that desire that often lead to the bad choices that are made at legal crossroads.

When thinking about money, it is worth asking yourself what types of emotions come into play when one considers breaking the law or doing something unethical to acquire more money. Is it jealousy, for example? Seeing someone else have nice things or get more money can trigger envy. And is envy an emotion that is healthy or fun to have? Is it good for you? Why act based on an unhealthy or bad emotion?

Other harmful emotions that drive a person to make poor legal decisions about money can include like feelings of insecurity, inadequacy, or a need to be liked. No one enjoys feeling so insecure, jealous, or unworthy of love and respect as a human being that only money can make a difference.

Remember that money is a factor in every aspect of day-to-day life. It takes money to buy groceries, to keep a car running to transport you to your job to earn more money, to keep clothes on your back, etc. So, every area of the law, in one form or another, also relates to money. One divides money in a divorce and uses it to pay child support. Money pays fines and court costs. Money is the reason for employment-law cases. Money is an ever-present factor both in legal decision making and in life. Remember to stay aware, and in balance, when it comes to making legal choices that are related to money.

MINIMIZING CONFLICT AND MAXIMIZING HARMONY

In life, engaging in conflict takes time and energy away from doing something productive or fun. Who wants to sit on the phone on hold for a long time trying to get a refund for an item because a voice in your head told you that the price was too good to be true? Who wants to take time off of work to go to the courthouse and pay a traffic fine because you just had to pass that car on the road, even if you knew that it involved speeding to do it? Who wants to go through the pain and hassle of a divorce just because you met someone whom you thought was attractive enough for a momentary fling? Most of the time, conflict is expensive, time-consuming, painful, and wasteful.

Still, there is plenty worth fighting for, and sometimes, conflict is unavoidable. The point is that when one faces a legal crossroad and exercises good legal decision making in order to keep balance in life, one often can avoid conflict or at least manage it much more effectively.

■ ■ ■

In summary, look at the sidebar below titled "Questions to Ask When Facing a Legal Crossroad." This is a list of suggested questions that you can ask yourself when confronted with the need to make a decision that can have legal consequences. Although every individual is in a particular place in life that is shaped by certain circumstances, this list of questions is meant as a basic framework of what to think about before making a choice about what direction you will go in when it comes time to choose a path.

The eleven questions that are posed in this list synthesize this chapter and its exercises. Let them serve as your better angel's voice when you are at a legal crossroad.

QUESTIONS TO ASK WHEN FACING A LEGAL CROSSROAD

1. Is what I am doing legal? If so, is it something that is personally ethical, and how will this impact me psychologically and spiritually? Will I be able to look myself in the mirror after this is done?

2. If I know a choice to be illegal, how will this potentially harm all involved? Me? My loved ones? Society?

3. What doors and opportunities might be closed off to me in the future if I do something that is not legal or ethical? Is a potential short-term gain worth the potential of long-term loss that could come from this?

4. How would my children see me after doing this if they knew about this choice I am considering? If I do not currently have children, how would children I might have in the future be impacted? Is this something I would be ashamed to tell my parents I am doing?

5. How *three-dimensionally aware* am I of this choice I am considering making? Have I thought about all the legal implications this decision has? What is the potential legal consequence of this decision?

6. How aware am I of the potential life imbalance this choice may cause me? Might this choice cause me to change my personality and thought patterns in a negative way? Will this give me the impression that this is OK, and that I can do more such things in the future?

7. Have I been asked to make a choice like this in the past? If so, what did I choose at that time? Why did I make that choice? What was the outcome then?

8. Was that similar choice I made in the past a good choice? Is it the reason I am in this personal reconstruction course today? Did I make the wrong choice then and, if I did, how did it cause me harm?

9. Have I made choices I regret in the past that were similar to the choice I am facing now? Did I commit to changing as a person then? Is this decision I am about to make consistent with the type of person I promised others and myself that I would be?

10. Does the choice I am about to make raise the possibility of conflict, or minimize it? If conflict, is it worth it? Might that conflict lead to having to make other bad choices down the line? If so, how bad might those choices be? Or is this path a path best avoided for the sake of balance in my life and a better legal future?

P A R T

III

INTEGRATION

In the previous parts of this book the reader was introduced to in-visioning and reconstruction tools, the methods and techniques useful for avoiding personal crashes and successfully managing the crises that cannot be avoided. This part presents the following topics to complete the process:

- A chapter to guide you in compiling your most important responses in the preceding exercises to create your In-visioning Life Plan; and,

- A final chapter that discusses how to implement your plan to move toward and remain in the life you invision.

8

PULL YOURSELF TOGETHER

Who looks outside, dreams;
who looks inside, awakes.

— Carl Gustav Jung

B Y THIS POINT in the book, you have hopefully worked through the previous chapters in order to in-vision your life as it has been, as it is now, and as you want it to be in the future. In doing so, you have worked through the exercises, and you have added the tools to your tool belt that will help you to reconstruct your life from the personal accident that may have derailed you. Now, you are at the point at which you begin to pull it all—and yourself—together.

This chapter begins your master recovery plan. The next chapter will focus on keeping you balanced so that you avoid future crashes and do better at managing the crises that you cannot avoid.

The only worksheet to use in this chapter compiles your prior exercise responses into a holistic plan of action. With just a little final effort, you can pull your values, feelings, and experiences together into a solid guide for your path forward.

GATHER THE PIECES

In reading this book and completing the exercises, you have gathered much information about yourself. You knew yourself before, but perhaps you had not systematically catalogued your thoughts, values, wants, goals, and personal resources. You are now ready to make use of them.

The worksheets that you used to capture information were introduced and related topics were presented, but not necessarily in the order that would be logical in a plan. Each worksheet is like a piece of a jigsaw puzzle that still needs to be assembled with other pieces in a particular order to reveal an image.

In the next exercise, you will organize the pieces—represented by the worksheets—into a coherent "In-Visioned Life Plan" (also referred to as "the plan" or "your plan"). An example of a completed plan is shown as Figure 8.1. The data for this example was taken from the fictitious "responses" in this book's illustrations of the many worksheets you were introduced to and encouraged to complete.

Exercise 8.1. Create your In-visioned Life Plan

This final exercise is about putting your worksheet responses into this final document. The first page of Figure 8.1 is a table of contents that is organized into four sections: your in-vision, risk-avoidance strategies, your crisis-management strategies and tools, and a "to-do" list of the actions that you need to take in order to realize your in-vision.

The reason for this organization is that it allows a logical methodology for managing risk and crises, as explained in the Risk Insights and Solutions Cycle (RISC)™ model (Island, 2018,

Figure 8.1. Completed In-visioned Life Plan

IN-VISIONED LIFE PLAN

A Roadmap to a Renewed Life

by Alex

TABLE OF CONTENTS

p. 22). The original RISC model was developed for organiza-
tions rather than for individual risk and crisis management, but
it has been adapted for our use in personal reconstruction as a

Completed In-visioned Life Plan (continued)

MY IN-VISION

Ref.: Appendix A.1. In-visioning your life

The following *guiding principles* reflect my life values, and they form the framework for my "in-vision" — the kind of life I want to work for and live going forward:

1. My kid is first priority. I cannot take work that takes me away from my kid for more than a few days or I'll miss visitation days.

2. Be a good provider. Earn enough to provide a good home and education for my child.

3. Spirituality grounds me now. I look forward to the Sunday services because I like the people, They forgive who I was and help me stay sober. I get good advice and support.

4. Money is not what I live for, but I need more income so I can stop living in debt.

5. Keep a good friendship with my soon-to-be ex. This is so I can get joint custody.

MY READYNESS FOR AVOIDING CRISES

Personal Risks

Ref.: Appendix A.2. Personal risk assessment

The following issues currently facing me represent the existing or potential problems that I need to manage over time. These are the issues that threaten my path toward my in-vision:

1. 2015 DUI arrest is keeping me from getting better work.

2. End-job earning low wages and soon will need to maintain two households.

3. Looming divorce. It could erupt into warfare if I'm not careful. I can't jeopardize joint custody of Adrian.

4. Credit card debt. Two credit cards that total $7,000 debt. I can hardly pay $200/mo.

5. Education loan debt of $10,000. Got ripped off by a diploma mill but bank still wants $

Personal Legal Stressors

Ref.: Appendix A.15. Legal stressors assessment

Stress is what can lead to depression, anger and discord between family, friends, and coworkers. The stress score below may be a "relationship survivability" predictor for me and my "significant other":

Score: 42 (0-64 Scale), so I can expect a stressed relationship unlikely to survive (40-52)

1

"Personal RISC" model, shown in Figure 8.2 on page 133.

The Personal RISC model is your roadmap to your in-visioned destination. Although we all hope to never have to get

Completed In-visioned Life Plan (continued)

Mitigation strategy: Selecting which stressor to mitigate first may depend on duration (the time needed to resolve) vs. criticality. I cannot try to mitigate all stressors at once. I will need to assess my stressors periodically (see ref.) to identify which stressor, compared to others, will significantly reduce the most tension in a relatively short time.

Fears That Diminish My Life

Ref.: Appendix A.10. Fears that diminish my life

I have certain fears that hinder me from fully experiencing life. The following are things I'd like to do, be, or overcome, but have found it difficult to do so:

1. Driving on highways, especially since the DUI accident.

2. I fear my child may follow in my footsteps. I need to stay clean, set a good example.

3. Public speaking. My AA group wants me to represent them at civic groups. Terrified!

Mitigation strategy: Generally, I may overcome a particular fear by desensitizing myself to it through repetitive, measured exposures to the fear. One small step at a time.

Anger-Management Skills

Ref.: Appendix A.7. How I deal with anger

Anger makes people act irrationally, impulsively and, in the end, regrettably. The anger management scores below are based on the three events I recalled and listed. According to this quick exercise/evaluation, I respond to stressful situations as follows:

Situational Diagnostic: 3 worse: my responses inflame situations

Emotional Diagnostic: 2 worse: my responses tend to hurt my well-being

Mitigation strategy: When faced with stressful situations that make me angry, I need to remember to WAIT UNTIL ANGER PASSES BEFORE ACTING. This may take minutes, hours, days or even weeks, but my response needs to wait until I am calm again.

Listening Skills

Ref.: Appendix A.9. Listening skills assessment

To engage in life is to "listen and respond" to others and my surroundings and—most of all—to my own inner voice. The listening skills I am most *deficient in and need to improve* are as follows:

1. Too busy too hear. I don't think through problems and shoot from the hip a lot.

2. Impatience. I don't devote enough time to things or hear people out. Get bored easily.

3. Don't like to be criticized. I shut people out unless I'm agreeing with what I'm hearing.

2

off the smoothly paved "Avoiding Crises" Highway (shown as a light grey rectangle), occasionally we are forced to detour and travel over rough terrain during "Reconstruction" (the white

Completed In-visioned Life Plan (continued)

Mitigation strategy: Actively pay attention to others when they speak and fight the urge to finish sentences for others or to interrupt with my own comments. Follow my conscience (what I feel is right) when moral, ethical, or legal issues are before me.

Past Legal Crossroads I Have Learned From

Ref.: Appendix A.14. Legal crossroads assessment

I have faced legal crossroads before that I now keep in mind to stay safe, legally. They are:

1. Control my temper (anger) to avoid jail, fines, or losing my parental rights or job.

2. Obey traffic rules and stay sober (no alcohol or drugs), especially on the road.

3. Stay "legal," as I don't want to miss out on my child's life growing up.

4. Pay bills and debts on time to avoid charges and bad credit ratings.

5. Don't justify a potentially illegal act (like cheating on taxes or insurance claims).

Planning for Disability or Old Age

Ref.: Appendices A11. How I use money, & A.13. Post-retirement resources plan

Calamity or decease can strike anyone at any time, and we all age. So it's never too soon (or too late) to plan for the "post-retirement" or "senior years" (they're not so "golden" for most people). So, my plan is detailed in the referenced appendix.

MY RESOURCES FOR MANAGING CRISES

Personal Strengths

Ref.: Appendix A.4. My positives inventory

The following are my personal strengths I can **consciously** employ to help me resolve this present crisis or future crashes (rather than act out of fear or anger):

1. I am intelligent. I'm a quick learner if I can get past being bored with things.

2. I am likable (when I'm sober and calm, not under the influence or angry)

3. I'm daring and willing to try new things (except for driving and public speaking)

Time Wasters to Avoid

Ref.: Appendix A.8. Using my time wisely

Time is valuable and limited, so I need to be aware of how I use it, and not waste it. The following is a list of ways in which I have wasted time in the past. I now resolve to stop:

3

rectangle at the bottom of Figure 8.2.). The detours are inevitable. We hope that our vehicle is built for the journey. A detailed tour of the Personal RISC roadmap is given in the next section.

Completed In-visioned Life Plan (continued)

1. Control my drinking and drug use so I don't miss work (lost wages) or get fired.

2. Don't look for "love" (dating sites) on the Internet. (Many wasted hours there.)

3. Don't waste time talking about emotional things like politics with strangers.

Past Useful Crisis Management Tools

Ref.: Appendix A.3. Former crises In my lfe

The following are tools I have used successfully in the past to manage personal crises:

1. Find support groups for issues like substance abuse, anger management, etc.

2. Use government and nonprofit groups for legal and financial assistance.

3. Join social groups to find healthy entertainment and exercise (all help with anger).

4. Join civic-minded groups to help others however I can (gets my mind off of me).

5. Get professional help (psychologists, finance advisors, etc.) to deal with problems.

People I Can Count On

Ref.: Appendix A.5. People in my life

Of the people I've listed in the appendix, the following three are my closest supporters:

1. My sister, Misty. She understands me better than mom. Gives me good advice.

2. Granpa Charlie. He's been through a lot of the same; gives me advice and support.

3. Dennis, my supervisor. Guides me at work and has stood by me at really bad times.

People Hurt by My Actions to Redeem

Ref.: Appendix A.6. People hurt by my actions

I have hurt the following people willfully (usually out of anger) or accidentally and plan to remedy my actions as follows:

Name	Hurtful Action	Problem Fix/Remedy
Tom Smith	Serious injuries from my accident	Borrow $ to pay his uninsured expenses
Mom	She'll feel responsible for the monetary damages	Show her I've handled the expenses so she won't worry
Uncle Charlie	Need to have him cosign my loan to pay for damages	Put his mind at ease by showing him payments are being made

4

To proceed, use the worksheet shown in Appendix A.16 on page 161. Fill in your plan with data from your completed worksheets using the following steps:

Completed In-visioned Life Plan (continued)

Realistic Budget for Financial Viability

Ref.: Appendix A11. How I use money & Appendix A.12. Monthly budget plan

Financial imbalance—in the form of burdensome debt or inadequate or no income to sustain my standard of living—may require an adjustment (downsizing) in material possessions and/or expenses.

Current budget status: I cannot make ends meet. I need professional help.

TO DO TOWARD MY IN-VISION

	Prio.	Describe the "To Do" Item	By When
☐	H	Keep going to AA to stay well (and keep visitation rights)	Ongoing
☐	H	Don't miss a single day of parental visitation with child	Ongoing
☐	L	Take up fishing with Adrian to get fresh air, fun and exercise	Ongoing
☐	M	To a County debt clinic (get on 4-year debt consolidation)	1/5/2018
☐	M	Get my DUI expunged by court so I can get better work	3/30/2018
☐	M	Join Toastmasters to learn public speaking, gain confidence	3/30/2018
☐	M	Take a trade school course, get licensed (better wages)	6/30/2018
☐	M	Get hired by a good company as tradesman and keep it	9/30/2018
☐	M	Start a pre-paid college fund for Adrian (once debts are paid)	2021?
☐	M	Open a retirement savings plan as soon as debts are paid	2021?
☐	L	Be the proud parent at Adrian's high school graduation	2027
☐	L	Be the proud parent at Adrian's college graduation	2031?
☐	M		
☐	M		
☐	M		

5

---

1. Get familiar with Figure 8.1, which is a self-explanatory illustration. The information to use in your plan is normally found in the last column to the right of the work-

sheets in the format of a table matrix, or toward the bottom of worksheets that include calculations or scoring.

2. Each section of your blank plan has a bolded header. The first line below the header refers to the corresponding worksheet for that section (e.g., "Ref.: Appendix A.2. Personal risk assessment" in the "Personal Risks" section).

3. Fit the information from the worksheet into the plan.

4. As you fill in the plan's sections, you should identify what you need to do to pursue your in-vision. Add those action items to the final section of your plan. Once your list is done, you may reorder these items in the chronological order in which they are due. This will result in an easy-to-understand plan of action—the activities that you have determined are important to do in order to move your in-vision forward.

Once you have your plan completed, you will be ready to take it for a spin, guided by the Personal RISC roadmap.

THE PERSONAL RISC ROADMAP

Think of your plan as your roadmap to your destination: your newly in-visioned life. Imagine that this map has a smooth, paved highway that is occasionally interrupted by potholes and detours into rough terrain that is under "reconstruction." If you drive too quickly, you will not be able to avoid the potholes, and you are likely to break something or have an accident. When you are detoured, the ground is likely to be difficult and at times may seem impassable. Don't be discouraged. Remember that the detours—the crises—are temporary and you can navigate your way back to the smooth, paved highway of life.

Understanding the Personal RISC Model

You should regard the Personal RISC model as a graphical version of your written plan. Think of them as two perspectives for the same thing, just like having a Google Maps printout with both the written directions as well as a copy of the actual map.

Essentially, the Personal RISC model has two parts: "The Before: Avoiding Crises," and "The After: Reconstruction." Let us examine them here.

The Before. This is what is known as *risk management*. It is represented by the light grey rectangle at the top of the model. It is the smooth highway of life. It is here that we take precautions in order to foresee and avoid accidents, and we learn "driving skills" such as anger management. Most importantly, it is in The Before that we place our hopes and plans for the future, even if they are not well thought-out. The Before has three components: in-visioning, early warning, and learning and adapting.

The cycle begins (and renews at the end of a cycle) when you create your in-vision—namely, the overarching, guiding principles that define your life goals and objectives. Your life goals should drive your early warning system (EWS), in that while you are creating tools and seeking resources to progress toward your goals, you are aware of threats and delays that could prevent you from reaching your life goals. This is much like with businesses that have strategic plans and goals. Such companies regularly conduct a test of their strengths, weaknesses, opportunities, and threats—commonly known as a SWOT analysis. You have to know your goals and be actively pursuing them to be able to register early warnings about problems that are approaching.

EWS includes activities like personal risk assessments and analyses of legal stressors and budgets. These forewarn you of weaknesses and holes in your plan that need attention before they deteriorate into a crisis.

Figure 8.2. Personal Risk Insights and Solutions Cycle

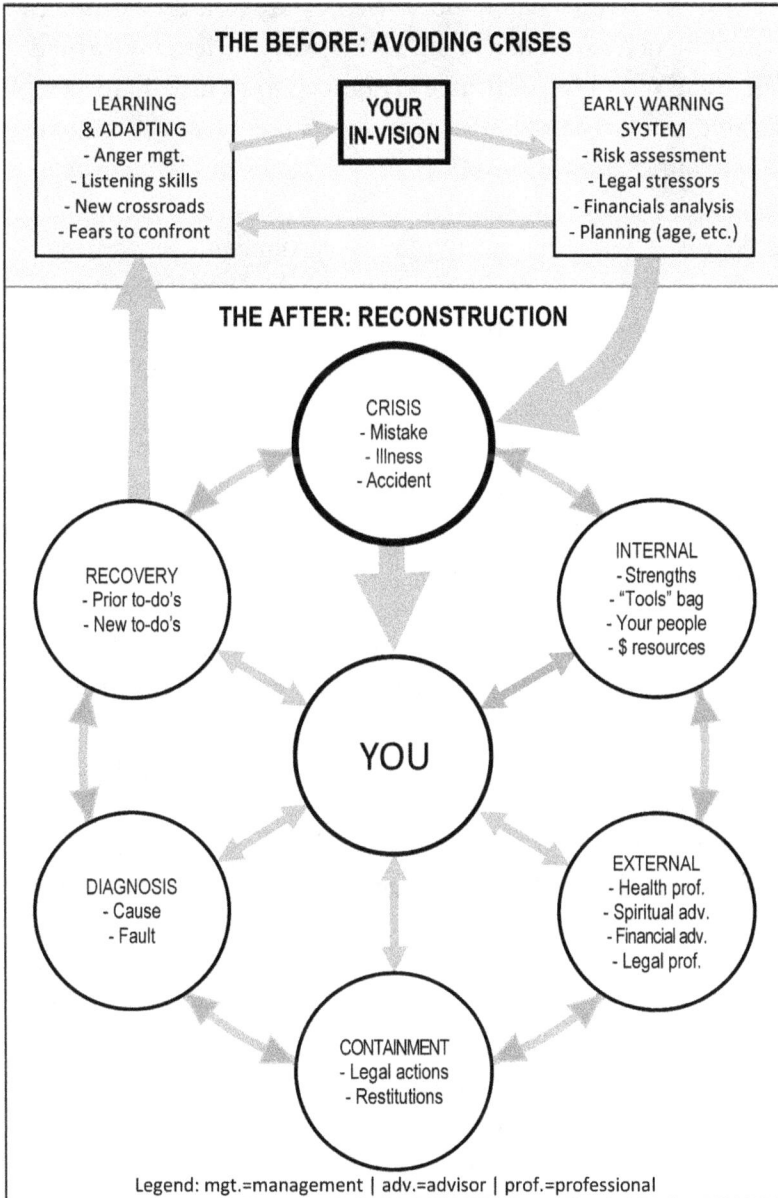

THE BEFORE: AVOIDING CRISES

LEARNING & ADAPTING	YOUR IN-VISION	EARLY WARNING SYSTEM
- Anger mgt.		- Risk assessment
- Listening skills		- Legal stressors
- New crossroads		- Financials analysis
- Fears to confront		- Planning (age, etc.)

THE AFTER: RECONSTRUCTION

CRISIS
- Mistake
- Illness
- Accident

RECOVERY
- Prior to-do's
- New to-do's

INTERNAL
- Strengths
- "Tools" bag
- Your people
- $ resources

YOU

DIAGNOSIS
- Cause
- Fault

EXTERNAL
- Health prof.
- Spiritual adv.
- Financial adv.
- Legal prof.

CONTAINMENT
- Legal actions
- Restitutions

Legend: mgt.=management | adv.=advisor | prof.=professional

Source: Island (2018). Adapted by permission from the publisher.

Ideally, weaknesses that you identify in the EWS phase are dealt with before they can happen. If they are not, they wind up having to be dealt with in a crisis. Either way, the lessons learned during the EWS phase or from a crisis need to be articulated and integrated into an updated plan in order to prevent the threat from repeating itself.

The After. A crisis may or may not be your fault, or anyone's fault. Many events are accidents or simply the inevitable results of living life and cannot be controlled. You may just be in the wrong place at the wrong time, or you may become gravely ill. Even self-induced crises are not always preventable. Human beings are fallible, so mistakes will be made—some small, others very serious. Everyone faces crises sooner or later, so we must be ready for the reconstruction part of the Personal RISC model.

Crises can happen even with the best risk assessment and management plan in place. Management does not mean elimination; it means taking steps to reduce the likelihood that the threat will be realized and, if it does, to have contingency strategies ready to minimize its effects and recover as quickly as possible with the least cost. Without a good plan, confusion will reign, and the remedy will not be available or will be very expensive.

For example, if you become seriously ill and have no health insurance you, then may still get medical treatment but at astronomical cost because as an individual you will not have group bargaining power to reduce medical costs, and you will be fully responsible for all bills, not just deductibles and copayments. Your choices surrounding this situation include having the foresight and resources to get health insurance before you needed it, foregoing medical treatment, or running up unaffordable bills (and probably going into bankruptcy). The list of possible crises that can visit individuals is long.

Using the Personal RISC Model

Negligence or criminal activity are self-induced crises that can be very costly. Such events can result in staggering emotional and financial stress from legal bills or loss of liberty. We can argue that justice favors the wealthy and is harsh on the underprivileged, but even well-known personalities like Johnny Depp, Robert Downey Jr., and Martha Stewart have found themselves on the wrong side of the law and have paid for it, financially and otherwise.

The reconstruction part of Figure 8.2 looks like a spoked wheel. Each of the circles represents a crisis-response phase. You may not pass through all of these phases in a particular crisis, but you are likely to employ many of them. As an example, you may not need to consult with an external resource, like a financial adviser, or to invoke containment measures like a restraining court order. But other phases are almost universally applicable.

In almost all cases, you will be able to diagnose the cause and fault of the crisis. If you cannot, however, then you won't be able to resolve the problem or learn lessons from it. The diagnostic phase also plays a significant role in reconstruction, when you identify and execute the actions that are needed for recovery.

What is certain is that severe crises are sure to force you through all The After phases for resolution. Understanding the Personal RISC roadmap will help you apply your In-visioned Life Plan and deal successfully with the stress of the crisis and the patience required to resolve it.

■ ■ ■

In summary, this chapter walks you through a final exercise in order to create your In-visioned Life Plan, which you can now use as a guide to reconstruct your life from the rubble of a crisis, or to work toward a set of goals that you might feel have been sidelined because of a lack of direction.

The concepts in this book might seem clear, and it may be easy to understand why they are worthwhile. The exercises may have brought you insight and clarity as well. It isn't until they see the light of day and are written on the paper in front of you that you see them for what they really are and can assess their accuracy and what needs to change. It is for this precise reason that reading a self-help book, by and large, does not bring lasting change. The information may make perfect sense as we read it, but if we don't also see our irrational beliefs and assumptions or have any insight into why we do what we do, then it won't be long before they will overpower the rational beliefs that this new information can help us to formulate and that we should use to change.

Now that you have a written plan and an EWS that focuses on your goals, you are prepared to move forward. You can refer to your plan as you go so that you don't have to remember each detail. Much like a teenage driver who starts out as a cautious and alert driver, it is easy to become less vigilant. After a year of driving, the teenager may become comfortable enough with his or her driving skills that they begin, for example, texting or trying to program the radio while driving. In an instant, the driver can be reminded about what a momentary loss of atten-tion can cause. Your written In-visioned Life Plan is your posted reminder about what can happen and what you should focus on, as well as where it is you're trying to reach.

C H A P T E R

9

A RENEWED YOU

*The road to wisdom? Well, it's plain and simple
to express: Err and err and err again but less and
less and less.*

— Piet Hein

IF YOU HAVE gone through this book and performed the
exercises, then you have already done the hard work of
in-visioning your life and—if you were experiencing a crisis—
planning and carrying out your personal reconstruction. This
is no small feat. It is one to be proud of. You have looked into
yourself in a way that few people dare to.

You may already be well along the path that you in-visioned
for your life plan, or you may be ready to start your personal
reconstruction. In either case, you now are on the road to a
renewed you. Your life plan should equip you to handle the road
hazards better than before.

This does not mean that you will not be confronted with new

crises, but you will likely face fewer surprises since your life plan probably lists potential future crises. Having identified these potential crises, you will be better prepared to deal with them, or even to avoid them. That alone may result in a happier life for you.

YOUR CHALLENGES NOW

We did not write this book to solve every problem that you may have had or might ever have, but rather we hoped that as you read the chapters and worked through the exercises that you would gain the necessary tools to look back, see where you may have made mistakes or gone off course, and then create a life plan that will allow you to go forward.

This book emphasizes that it is not helpful to focus only on our past mistakes without thinking about where we want to go and how we shall get there. The American musician Brad Paisley once stated, "If you make the mistake of looking back too much, you aren't focused enough on the road in front of you." This book is not merely about looking back or looking at our past mistakes, but also looking forward to the future that we wish to construct. In the end, what was cannot be changed, but you have the ability to seize your future and make it what you desire.

WHAT YOU HAVE LEARNED ABOUT YOURSELF

One way to avoid many personal crises and improve your life is to learn how to control your emotions. Emotions may cause us to act impulsively or irrationally. On one hand, undue ebullience or optimism, for example, could lead us to buy things impulsively, to buy things that we cannot afford, or to make agreements without clearly examining what we are committing to. Later, we may come to regret such choices.

On the other hand, anger often leads us and others into

troubled waters. Anger is an emotion that is often responsible for some of the worst crises—and crimes—in life.

Everyone feels anger from time to time. Some people live most of their lives feeling constant anger. Most of us will recognize that the worst mistakes that we have made probably occurred in a fit of rage. Your life plan may well have a section that is devoted to learning about how to deal with anger. Does that mean that you can learn to live without anger? No. All normal humans will feel anger and, yes, there is a place for righteous anger. What is important, then, is not what we feel but knowing how to use and control our feelings. Small children are aware of their feelings, but mature adults not only know what they feel but how to control and act on those feelings. To be an adult, then, is to learn to control one's emotions and actions.

Fear is another emotion that can affect you negatively. Fear may be justified but, like anger, fear may also cause you to act irrationally or impulsively. Just as in the case of anger, we need to control fear so that it becomes a warning tool rather than the cause of an overreaction. Depending on what causes the fear, we may best manage it by not acting thoughtlessly while in its grip. Conversely, certain fears may be controlled by purposely facing them in measured exposures. This, too, should now become part of your life plan.

One of the most difficult skills is learning to listen to your own inner voice. Hearing yourself—listening to your inner voice—is a necessary skill for improving your life and avoiding crises. If you feel that something is wrong, trust your gut, listen to yourself, and realize that your inner self is asking you to stay away from that action, situation, or person.

Listening to yourself does not mean that you should discount or ignore what others may be saying to you. It is not easy to hear others, absorb what they say, and learn from them. This skill is truly difficult to learn or improve, but it will improve your relations with family, friends, coworkers, and people you just meet.

You may be familiar with the saying that "God gave us two ears and one mouth because we should listen twice as much as we speak." It is no secret that you will learn more by listening to what others say than by talking.

By means of these exercises, you may also have defined what harm or hurt you may have caused not only yourself, but also others. If you have not already done so, now is the time to make amends. This could be a principle trait of the renewed you. What you do for others without prodding or without a particular reason will leave a good mark in their view of you and in your view of yourself, too. If your actions for the good of others are done not to make amends but simply to engender goodwill, then all the better. The objects of your acts of kindness will be part of your network in a time of crisis. But be sure to listen to them in their times of crisis.

ALONG THE THOUSAND-MILE JOURNEY

You began that proverbial thousand-mile journey when you opened and began to read this book. That was the first step. In reading through its chapters and completing the exercises, you took many more steps toward your destination—the fulfillment of your in-visioned life plan.

You are now well along the road to reconstructing your life and to recovery, if you are still working through a crisis, or to improvement if you simply want to improve your life and the lives of those with whom you have or shall come in contact.

Many sections of the life plan that you have constructed may change over time as your life circumstances change. But the principle tenets in your life plan—as expressed in the first section of the life plan—are unlikely to change much, as they are—or should be—a reflection of your core values. The rest of the plan just defines the issues that surround those values, identifies the resources that you can count on to pursue your life goals, and lists the actions that you need to take in order to realize your life plan.

It is our sincere desire that, after reading this book, you will have come to the realization that no matter what has happened in the past, you can shape tomorrow into a future about which you can be proud.

Additionally, just as a police officer tries to reconstruct an accident, we too need to ask ourselves such questions as:

- Was I going too quickly in life?
- Was I up against something bigger than I?
- Were drugs or alcohol involved in my going off-course?
- How did I damage myself and others?
- How do I use my past to shape my future?

These are the first questions of an in-visioning plan.

Now that you have read the book, go back and ask yourself these questions again. Are your answers the same as when you first began to read this book? How are they different?

This book offers you ideas for your personal in-visioning plan. We hope that we have given you, the reader, ideas about how to improve the quality of your life. Remember, the best way to solve a crisis is to avoid it! You can avoid most crises by simply following the four main principles in this book:

. . . listen to your inner voice

. . . learn to control fear and anger

. . . manage your finances well, and

. . . think carefully when you are at a legal crossroad.

P A R T

IV

APPENDICES

This section contains the worksheets that help the reader gather, analyze and act on his or her personal information. The worksheets are, effectively, the users' in-visioning and reconstruction "tools."

VISIT QUEST-PUBLISHING.COM TO DOWNLOAD FREE FULL (U.S. LETTER) SIZE VERSIONS OF THE WORK-SHEETS SHOWN IN THIS BOOK.

A P P E N D I X

A

EXERCISE WORKSHEETS

THIS APPENDIX PROVIDES the exercise worksheets in blank form. The worksheets in this book can be photocopied for individual use, but you may find it easier to download them at no cost from the publisher's website at www.quest-publishing. com/resources/personal-reconstruction.

The electronic versions of the exercise worksheets available online are in full U.S. letter-size (8.5"X11"), giving users more space to work with. They are in *rich text format* (.rtf), which can be opened in most any word processor for printing.

Two of the downloadable .rtf forms ae also available for download as Microsoft Excel spreadsheets that are programmed to perform the mathematical calculations for the user:

- Monthly budget plan
- Post-retirement resources plan.

These two spreadsheets are the electronic versions of the paper forms found in this section as "Appendix A.12. Monthly budget plan" on page 157 and "Appendix A.13. Post-retirement resources plan" on page 158.

Appendix A.1. In-visioning my life

Major Question	Minor Questions	Life Journey Risk	Guiding Principle

Appendix A.2. Personal risk assessment

Type and Description of Risk	Risk Level	Expected Duration

Appendix A.3. Former crises in my life

Crisis	Tools I Used to Get Back On My Feet

Appendix A.4. My positives inventory

1	
2	
3	
4	
5	
6	
7	
8	
9	
10	

Appendix A.5. People in my life

	Name	Positive	Negative
FAMILY			
FRIENDS			
COLLEAGUES			
ACQUAINTANCES			
PASSERSBY			

Appendix A.6. People hurt by my action

ERROR/FAULT:			
Names of People Hurt	Direct or Indirect	How	Action To Be Taken To Fix the Problem

Appendix A.7. How I deal with anger

Anger Trigger (What Made You Mad?)	Your Response	The Situational Outcome			Your Emotional Outcome		
		Better	Same	Worse	Better	Same	Worse
TOTALS							

Remember that this is only a "quick-and-dirty" exercise and not a true psychological/personality test. It is for your own use as a way to begin to articulate and understand yourself and your behavior.

INSTRUCTIONS:
1. List the **last** three instances you remember in which you were seriously angered by someone or something (e.g., getting reprimanded at work or school, a loud argument with your spouse/friend, etc.)
2. Enter how you responded (e.g., tried to reason, insulted back, threw something, etc.)
3. Check an option in the situational block to indicate what the outcome to your response was.
4. Check an option in the emotional block to indicate how you felt about it after your response.
5. Total each column to see what your behavior tends to be in anger-inducing situations.

SITUATIONAL DIAGNOSTIC (people generally interpret the results in the following fashion):
3 Better outcomes = You believe your responses work for you in defusing stressful situations.
3 Worse outcomes = You recognize your responses are inflammatory to stressful situations.

EMOTIONAL DIAGNOSTIC (people generally interpret the results in the following fashion):
3 Better outcomes = Your responses generally alleviate your stress (they work for you).
3 Worse outcomes = Your responses are self-injurious (they hurt your emotional well-being).

Responses in-between (usually 2's) are "trending" to the response category where most points are.

Appendix A.8. Using my time wisely

Your "Sin" (Missed Mark)	Negative Life Impact

Personal Reconstruction

Appendix A.9. Listening skills assessment

Obstacle	What Stops You
Too much noise in our lives	
Fear of quiet	
Too busy to hear	
Impatience	
Fear of change	
Fear of being unworthy	
Fear of the answer	

Appendix A.10. Fears that diminish my life

My Fear	How It Diminishes My Life

Appendix A.11. How I use money

Main Monetary Expenses	What These Expenses Symbolize

Appendix A.12. Monthly budget plan

SAVINGS GOALS			
Purpose	Total To Save	Save By	Monthly Amount
Total Monthly Savings			

INCOME		
Source/Description	Receive By	Amount
Total Monthly Income		

Minus

EXPENSES		
Description	Due Date	Amount
Total Expenses		

Minus

Savings Monthly Amount	

Equals

Monthly Balance	

Surplus (+) = Disposable income | Deficit (-) = Budget adjustment needed to equal at least 0 or a positive number

This worksheet is available as a Microsoft Excel spreadsheet from quest-publishing.com/resources/personal-reconstruction.

Appendix A.13. Post-retirement resources plan

Potential Issues	Mitigating Strategy	Desired Outcome

Retirement Resources Needed	Manner of Acquisition	Planned For Savings
Subtotal of Planned Retirement Resources Needed		

Minus

Personal Savings/Investments	Manner of Acquisition	Current Savings
Subtotal of Current Retirement Resources		

Equals

CURRENT SHORTFALL	
TIME LEFT TO RETIRE/ACCRUE THROUGH FOLLOWING:	

Employer/Govt. Annuities	Manner of Acquisition	Expected Value
Subtotal of Sponsored Plans		

Plus

Yearly retirement income distribution of 5% from Retirement Resources	
TOTAL PLANNED RETIREMENT INCOME (PRESENT VALUE)	

This worksheet is available as a Microsoft Excel spreadsheet from quest-publishing.com/ resources/personal-reconstruction.

Appendix A.14. Legal crossroads assessment

Use this form to create a list of legal crossroads you have faced	
Bad choices made (or wanted to do but did not) while at a legal crossroad	Negative consequences (lost opportunities and other costs) that resulted (or would have) from bad choices

Appendix A.15. Legal stressors assessment

ISSUE	YOU	YOUR PARTNER
Child custody/child support		
Opening a new business, starting a new job, going back to school, or a new career path		
Major physical or psychological medical challenge		
Major credit or financial change/challenge		
Criminal case or incarceration		
Having to care for or be a guardian for relatives outside the nuclear family		
Serious debt or bankruptcy		
Children from previous relationship is/are facing challenges		
INDIVIDUAL SCORES		
COMBINED SCORE		

Scale:	0 = None / 1 =Maybe / 2 = Possible / 3 = Probable / 4 = Certain
Scoring:	0 to 13 points = no forecasted stressors for the relationship
	14 to 26 points = expect some points of contention to work through
	27 to 39 points = expect a need to overcome manageable issues
	40 to 52 points = expect a very stressed relationship unlikely to survive
	53 plus points = expect a highly challenged relationship very unlikely to survive

Appendix A.16. In-visioned life plan

-

IN-VISIONED LIFE PLAN

A Roadmap to a Renewed Life

by _____

TABLE OF CONTENTS

In-visioned Life Plan (continued)

MY IN-VISION

Ref.: Appendix A.1. In-visioning your life

The following *guiding principles* reflect my life values, and they form the framework for my "in-vision" — the kind of life I want to work for and live going forward:

1. _____
2. _____
3. _____
4. _____
5. _____

MY READYNESS FOR AVOIDING CRISES

Personal Risks

Ref.: Appendix A.2. Personal risk assessment

The following issues currently facing me represent the existing or potential problems that I need to manage over time. These are the issues that threaten my path toward my in-vision:

1. _____
2. _____
3. _____
4. _____
5. _____

Personal Legal Stressors

Ref.: Appendix A.15. Legal stressors assessment

Stress is what can lead to depression, anger and discord between family, friends, and coworkers. The stress score below may be a "relationship survivability" predictor for m and my "significant other":

Score: ___, so I can expect _____

Mitigation strategy: Selecting which stressor to mitigate first may depend on duration (the time needed to resolve) vs. criticality. I cannot try to mitigate all stressors at once.

In-visioned Life Plan (continued)

will need to assess my stressors periodically (see ref.) to identify which stressor, compared to others, will significantly reduce the most tension in a relatively short time.

Fears That Diminish My Life

Ref.: Appendix A.10. Fears that diminish my life

I have certain fears that hinder me from fully experiencing life. The following are things I'd like to do, be, or overcome, but have found it difficult to do so:

1. _____

2. _____

3. _____

Mitigation strategy: Generally, I may overcome a particular fear by desensitizing myself to it through repetitive, measured exposures to the fear. One small step at a time.

Anger-Management Skills

Ref.: Appendix A.7. How I deal with anger

Anger makes people act irrationally, impulsively and, in the end, regrettably. The anger management scores below are based on the three events I recalled and listed. According to this quick exercise/evaluation, I respond to stressful situations as follows:

Situational Diagnostic: _____

Emotional Diagnostic: _____

Mitigation strategy: When faced with stressful situations that make me angry, I need to remember to WAIT UNTIL ANGER PASSES BEFORE ACTING. This may take minutes, hours, days or even weeks, but my response needs to wait until I am calm again.

Listening Skills

Ref.: Appendix A.9. Listening skills assessment

To engage in life is to "listen and respond" to others and my surroundings and—most of all—to my own inner voice. The listening skills I am most *deficient in and need to improve* are as follows:

1. _____

2. _____

3. _____

In-visioned Life Plan (continued)

Mitigation strategy: Actively pay attention to others when they speak, and fight the urge to finish sentences for others or to interrupt with my own comments. Follow my conscience (what I feel is right) when moral, ethical, or legal issues are before me.

Past Legal Crossroads I Have Learned From

Ref.: Appendix A.14. Legal crossroads assessment

I have faced legal crossroads before that I now keep in mind to stay safe, legally. They are:

1. _____

2. _____

3. _____

4. _____

5. _____

Planning for Disability or Old Age

Ref.: Appendices A11. How I use money & A.13. Post-retirement resources plan

Calamity or decease can strike anyone at any time, and we all age. So it's never too soon (or too late) to plan for the "post-retirement" or "senior years" (they're not so "golden" for most people). So, my plan is detailed in the referenced appendix.

MY RESOURCES FOR MANAGING CRISES

Personal Strengths

Ref.: Appendix A.4. My positives inventory

The following are my personal strengths that I can **consciously** employ to help me resolve this present crisis or future crashes (rather than act out of fear or anger):

1. _____

2. _____

3. _____

Time Wasters to Avoid

Ref.: Appendix A.8. Using my time wisely

In-visioned Life Plan (continued)

Time is valuable and limited, so I need to be aware of how I use it, and not waste it. The following is a list is of ways in which I have wasted time in the past. I now resolve to avoid these time wasters so I can focus on important things:

1. _____

2. _____

3. _____

Past Useful Crisis Management Tools

Ref.: Appendix A.3. Former crises in my life

The following are tools I have used successfully in the past to manage personal crises:

1. _____

2. _____

3. _____

4. _____

5. _____

People I Can Count On

Ref.: Appendix A.5. People in my life

Of the people I've listed in the appendix, the following three are my closest supporters:

1. _____

2. _____

3. _____

People Hurt by My Actions to Redeem

Ref.: Appendix A.6. People hurt by my actions

I have hurt the following people willfully (usually out of anger) or accidentally and plan to remedy my actions as follows:

Name	Hurtful Action	Problem Fix/Remedy
_____	_____	_____
_____	_____	_____
_____	_____	_____

In-visioned Life Plan (continued)

Realistic Budget for Financial Viability

Ref.: Appendices A11. How I use money & A.12: Monthly budget plan

Financial imbalance—in the form of burdensome debt or inadequate or no income to sustain my standard of living—may require an adjustment (downsizing) in material possessions and/or expenses.

Current budget status: _____

TO DO TOWARD MY IN-VISION

Prio.	Describe the "To Do" Item	By When
☐		
☐		
☐		
☐		
☐		
☐		
☐		
☐		
☐		
☐		
☐		
☐		
☐		
☐		

Works Cited

"Belief-O-Matic®." (n.d.). Beliefnet. Accessed August 29, 2017. http://www.beliefnet.com/entertainment/quizzes/beliefomatic.aspx.

Boym, Svetlana. 2002. *The Future of Nostalgia*. New York: Basic Books.

Descartes, René. 1987. *Discourse on the Method of Rightly Conducting the Reason*. Translated by Elizabeth S. Haldane and G. R. T. Ross. In *Great Books of the Western World*, vol. 31, edited by Mortimer J. Adler. Chicago: Encyclopedia Britannica, Inc.

Farabee, Mike. (2001). "Laws of Thermodynamics." Estrella Mountain Community College. Accessed September 20, 2017. https://www2.estrellamountain.edu/faculty/farabee/biobk/BioBookEner1.html#Table%20of%20Contents.

Freeman, Arthur, and Rose DeWolf. (1990). *Woulda, Coulda, Shoulda: Overcoming Regrets, Mistakes, and Missed Opportunities*. New York: HarperPerennial.

Gladwell, Malcolm. 2013. *Outliers: The Story of Success*. New York: Back Bay Books.

Greenburg, Dan, and Marcia Jacobs. 1987. *How to Make Yourself Miserable: Another Vital Training Manual*. New York: Random House.

Hobbes, Thomas. 2012. *Leviathan*, vol. 3. Edited by Noel Malcolm. Oxford: Clarendon Press.

Island, Jacques. 2018. *Your Plan Is Your Parachute: A Simplified Guide to Business Continuity and Crisis Management.* Miami, Fla.: Quest Publishing.

Laplanche, Jean, and Jean-Bertrand Pontalis. 1988. *The Language of Psychoanalysis.* London: Karnac Books.

Lawrence, D. H. 1930. *Pansies.* London: Secker.

Maranjian, Selena. 2007. "Are You Worrying or Acting?" *The Motley Fool.* Accessed December 3, 2017. https://www.fool.com/retirement/2007/04/30/are-you-worrying-or-acting.aspx.

Salerno, Steve. 2005. *Sham: How the Self-Help Movement Made America Helpless.* New York: Crown.

Stevenson, Robert Louis. 2017. *The Strange Case of Dr. Jekyll and Mr. Hyde and Other Stories.* London: Macmillan Collector's Library.

Sylvester, David Hale. 2012. *Traveling at the Speed of Life.* United States: Contribute2.

Tolle, Eckhart. 2008. *A New Earth: Awakening to Your Life's Purpose.* New York: Penguin.

Walsch, Neale Donald. 1999. *Conversations with God.* Charlottesville, Va.: Hampton Roads.

Wang, Jim. 2017 "Best Personal Finance Software Apps of 2017." *Wallet Hacks.* Accessed September 1, 2017. https://wallethacks.com/best-personal-finance-software-apps/.

Index

different perspectives of, 58
meaning of, 57
EWS. *See* early warning system
expectations, 56

F

family and matrimonial law, 109
fear, 74, 77, 139
finances. *See also* reconstruction:
    financial
    and handling money, 8, 80,
        95–96, 141
    and saving, 81, 95
    as an aspect of life, 7
    financial goals, 80, 87
    learning about, 80
    planning tools
        online, 97–99
        traditional paper-based, 100

G

God
    and personal reconstruction, xv
    notions of, xv, 71, 76
golden years. *See* retirees
Gremlin automobile, the, 57
guilt. *See also* internal Stockholm
        syndrome
    denial of, 31
    for mistakes made, 52
    manipulative, 55
    motivational, 32
    nonuseful, 55
    self-blame, 52
    tendency to over-emphasize, 31
    useful, 55

H

happiness, 42
    as a personal choice, 51
harmony, maximizing, 119

human
    collision factors, 21–24
    error, xvi, 36

I

importance, risk levels
    , 20
inmates, 10
insight, 49
internal Stockholm syndrome, 55
investing, 92
in-visioning
    and the law, 106
    as a RISC model component, 132
    concept, xiii
    definition, xviii, 4
    for finances, 80
    your life, 16, 124

L

law. *See* civil law; *See* criminal law;
        See employment law; *See* fam-
        ily and matrimonial law
    and conflict, minimizing, 119
    and harmony, maximizing, 119
    and legal decisions, 110, 117
    and legal problems, 106, 108
    and money, 117–118
    and representation, 107
    as an aspect of life, 7
    in our lives, 101–120
    origins of, 102
    views of law, 9
learning, 132, 141
legal. *See* law
legal crossroad. *See* crossroad, legal
level, risk, 20–21
life
    highway of, 14–25
    in-visioned, 16–19, 124–131
    plan, 124–131

levels, 20
  consequences, 20
  importance, 20
  probability, 20
management, 132–134
  types, 20
Risk Insights and Solutions Cycle,
    124. *See also* Before, The
roles, 58
  as religion, 59

S

self-awareness, 60
self-blame, 52
sin, 69
spirituality
  and human beings, 9–11
  and money, 74
  as an aspect of life, 6
  as an opportunity v. obligation, 69
  defined, 68, 76
  in a community, 76
  practicing, 69
    through prayer, 71
    through work, 71
spiritual wellness, 67–78
Stockholm syndrome, internal.
    See internal Stockholm syn-
    drome
strengths, 37

T

teenagers. *See* adolescents
temporal reality, 25
The After. *See* After, The
The Before. *See* Before, The
thermodynamics, 24
time
  and finances, 80
  using wisely, 70, 77
type, risk, 20–21

V

validation, 60, 86

W

work, 71, 87

About the Authors

Peter Tarlow, Ph.D.

Dr. Peter E. Tarlow is a world-renowned speaker and expert specializing in the impact of crime and terrorism on the tourism industry, event and tourism risk management, and tourism and economic development. He was also the director and rabbi of Texas A&M Hilel for thirty years. Upon retirement he assumed the leadership of the Center for Latino – Jewish Relations. Peter writes a weekly bilingual social religious commentary that is read throughout the United States and Latin American and he also writes a monthly philosophy column for the Bryan Eagle. Peter has been a chaplain for the College Station police department since 1988 In April of 2013, he was asked to accept the role as the Envoy for the Office of Chancellor of the Texas A&M system, John Sharp. In 2015 he began teaching at the Texas A&M Medical School's Department of Humanities, and in 2016, Governor Gregg Abbot of Texas named him as the Chairman of the Texas Holocaust and Genocide Commission.

Tom Marrs, Ph.D.

Dr. Tom Marrs grew up in a heavy equipment salvage yard in the small central Texas town of Rockdale. From an early age he had an affinity for the question "why?" which has driven his exploration of human behavior and commonalities in what causes people to get into life crashes. A licensed psychologist, Tom spent 12 years as one of two clinicians providing counseling to over 10,000 employees and their dependents at the Texas A&M University Employee Assistance Program. Tom now has a private practice, and is a human resources specialist, serendipitously, for the Texas A&M Transportation Institute. In his spare time, Tom enjoys travelling with his wife and son, and teaching interpersonal psychology at the Center for Executive Development at the Texas A&M Mays School of Business.

Nathaniel Tarlow, J.D.

Nathaniel "Nate" Tarlow is an attorney and owner of the law firm Tarlow Legal Associates, LLP in Houston, Texas. His practice focuses on criminal defense, and some civil and administrative law matters. Nate's initial working years in a Nevada casino and as a bilingual tour guide at Hoover Dam taught him the value and importance of good people skills and interacting productively with racially, culturally, and socioeconomically diverse people. As a law student he clerked at a Texas District Court of Appeals, and was awarded the American Jurisprudence Award twice. In 2004 he graduated from South Texas College of Law and in 2008 he was honored as one of the top 10 heroes of the Republic of Honduras by the "El Heraldo" newspaper for a legal victory involving a deported Honduran citizen. Nate enjoys scuba diving and the outdoors, and travels the world to learn about law and tourism and how it affects local economies and customs.

Eduardo Leite, Ph.D.

Dr. Eduardo Leite, a business and management expert, began his professional life as a soccer player with such notable Portuguese football clubs as Gil Vicente, Desportivo das Aves, Feirense, Sanjoanense and Arrifanense. After retiring from professional sports he went on into business and doctoral research, focusing on management, entrepreneurship, and business finance. Eduardo lived through Portugal's recent Great Recession, an economic depression the likes of the U.S.' Great Depression of 1929. Those hard economic times forced Eduardo and many of his fellow Portuguese to recover through personal reconstruction. He earned a masters' degree in business administration in 2003, and a doctorate in management (finance) in 2007 from the *Universidade de Trás-os-Montes Alto Douro* in Vila Real, Portugal. He coauthored *Decisões de Investimento* ("Investment Decisions"), a book on personal finance. Eduardo is married and has three children.

Acknowledgments

This book's authors want to acknowledge the men and women of police departments throughout the world whose concepts concerning accident reconstruction inspired us to write this book. We also realize that we would not have been able to succeed in this endeavor without the loving support of our families and their willingness to "sacrifice time" with us so we could accomplish this goal. Finally we wish to acknowledge Jacques Island and his Quest Publishing colleagues without whose support this project would never have come to fruition.